JOHN
WESLEY

JOHN
WESLEY

His Life and Thought

Timothy J. Crutcher

BEACON HILL PRESS
OF KANSAS CITY

Copyright © 2015 by Timothy J. Crutcher and Beacon Hill Press of Kansas City
Beacon Hill Press of Kansas City
PO Box 419527
Kansas City, MO 64141
www.BeaconHillBooks.com

ISBN 978-0-8341-3494-2

Printed in the
United States of America

Cover Design: John Yuelkenbeck, Alias Creative Group
Interior Design: Sharon Page
Cover Image: Bridwell Library Special Collections, Perkins School of Theology, Southern Methodist University

Library of Congress Cataloging-in-Publication Data
Crutcher, Timothy J.
    John Wesley : his life and thought / Timothy J. Crutcher.
        pages cm
    Includes bibliographical references.
    ISBN 978-0-8341-3494-2 (pbk.)
    1. Wesley, John, 1703-1791. 2. Methodist Church—England—Clergy—Biography. I. Title.
    BX8495.W5C795 2015
    287.092—dc23
    [B]
                                                                2014035221

Scripture quotations marked KJV are from the King James Version.
Scripture quotations marked NKJV are from the *New King James Version* (NKJV). Copyright © 1979, 1980, 1982 Thomas Nelson, Inc. Used by permission.

The Internet addresses, email addresses, and phone numbers in this book are accurate at the time of publication. They are provided as a resource. Beacon Hill Press of Kansas City does not endorse them or vouch for their content or permanence.

10 9 8 7 6 5 4

To my students and colleagues at
Southern Nazarene University

Contents

Introduction

John Wesley is a significant theological figure for many people in the Protestant church, particularly for those who own the legacy of his Methodist movement and who attend one of the various denominations that have arisen from it. This book is an attempt to give the reader a basic orientation to both John Wesley's biography and to the most significant parts of his theological legacy. It is intended as an easy introduction to this rather complex figure, and so it is a book primarily designed for beginning students of Wesley in courses of ministerial preparation or for interested laypeople who would like to know more about this great thinker and evangelist. It is, therefore, a book more oriented toward the church than the formal academy. Hopefully, however, it is a book that can serve as a bridge between the two by giving readers enough "thinking handles" on Wesley that they can profitably engage deeper and more scholarly works about the man.

In part I of this book, we will introduce Wesley's biography, beginning with an overview of his historical setting and then looking at his childhood, his early adulthood, the events that began his ministry, the earliest decade of the Evangelical Revival of which he was a part and finishing with two chapters on the later sections of his life. In this brief biographical glimpse, we will try to balance both the personal details of Wesley's own life and the way his life and ministry fit into the larger controversies and issues with which he engaged.

In part II of the book, we will explore the basic intuitions that consistently emerge throughout his sermons and other writings. Wesley was what we might call an occasional theologian, meaning that he performed his theological vocation as the occasion demanded it—a little bit here, a little bit there; here a sermon, there a small tract. He never organized all of that into a systematized theology himself, and so all patterns we might use to organize his thought are somewhat artificial. However, organize we must, so our presentation of Wesley will begin with his theological method and then explore his basic views of God, creation, human beings, and sin. With this background, we will turn to Wesley's portrayal of the great drama of salvation—both in general and in a specific "order of salvation"—and how that salvation works its way out in the corporate life of the church.

Because this book is intended as a simple introduction, we should note at the outset that Wesley's life and thought are, in fact, more complicated than they are here presented. In trying to capture the major events of his life and the major intuitions that drive his thought, many layers of nuance had to be ignored. This is, of course, where we must start when we begin our journey of learning in any area, but it helps to be reminded of that up front, lest the reader think that anything said or claimed in this book should be taken as the last word on the subject. The goal of this book is to make the big picture as clear as possible, and so we have ignored some of the complexities that would easily cloud that picture. So, while we believe that Wesley's theological vision is coherent, we can admit that Wesley's implementation of that vision in his various writings and activities was not always so coherent. However, those inconsistencies are easier to see against the backdrop of a larger vision of his work. And while they ought to concern historians and systematic theologians of our own day, they can be conveniently ignored by those just starting out on their encounter with Wesley.

Since this introduction is intended as a primary encounter with Wesley, we have focused much more on his own writings—particularly his *Journal* and his sermons—than on what other people have said about him. References outside of Wesley have been kept to a minimum, and all citations are from Wesley unless explicitly stated otherwise. In citing Wesley, we have tried to give enough information for the reader to find the quote in any edition of his work, but we have also included, where available, volume and page citations in parentheses (for example, "(8:13)") for the Bicentennial Edition of Wesley's works (*The Works of John Wesley* [Oxford University Press and Abingdon Press, 1980–2013]). When complete, this will be the standard edition of Wesley's works in English. For those works that are yet unavailable in that edition, we have cited the previous standard editions of Wesley's works. We will cite *The Works of John Wesley* (3rd edition, edited by Thomas Jackson [Kansas City: Beacon Hill Press of Kansas City, 1978]) as "Jackson," with the volume and page number. For his later letters, we will use *The Letters of the Rev. John Wesley, A.M.* (edited by John Telford [London: Epworth, 1931]) and cite that as "Telford," also with volume and page number. In any quote from Wesley, the reader may assume that all emphases and italics come from Wesley's published originals.

Finally, we should mention a feature of our use of language that some English readers might find odd, namely the attempt to avoid gender-biased language—particularly when referring to God. This means we will not use any pronouns for God, always referring to God as God and not with designations such as "he" or "him." It may sound unnatural, but then using human language to talk about God is already unnatural in some way. Perhaps the awkwardness of talking about what God does for God's self or the way God feels about God's creation will remind us that God does not fit nicely and neatly in our premade human categories of thought or language. Wesley, of course, lived in a time before such concerns arose, and we have made no attempt to conform Wesley's writings to our contemporary sensitivities. He will use masculine pronouns for God, and say "man," "mankind," and "he" when referring to generic persons. Perhaps we should be bothered by such things, but we will just have to forgive him and his culture for their blindness up front. This seems better than constantly calling attention to it with designations such as "[sic]."

This, then, is our road map, a brief orientation toward the exploration ahead of us. However, road maps only really matter if we follow them, so let us begin the journey.

PART I
JOHN WESLEY'S LIFE

one

Wesley's Eighteenth-Century England

To understand a writer like John Wesley—or any writer from the past, for that matter—it helps to understand something of the environment in which he or she lived and wrote. Meaning is always a function of context, and so we often need to put writers in their historical context to figure out what they meant—especially ones who lived centuries before we were born. The world to which they wrote was different from ours. It had different struggles, different values, and different blind spots. Knowing something about those differences helps us to hear what those writers were saying more clearly. Of course, we do the work of history with much "fear and trembling," since we cannot claim to understand even our own context perfectly. If we don't understand all the things that shape how we think and act today, we are not likely to get everything right about a time that is now only available to us through documents and artifacts. Still, even our imperfect attempts at understanding John Wesley's historical context should prevent some of the mistakes we would make if we tried to read him as though he were writing today. Sometimes it is our distance and difference from those writers that make them most helpful to us, and understanding that distance brings their work into clearer focus.

John Wesley lived from 1703 until 1791 in England, the country occupying the southeast half of the island of Britain. The eighteenth century was a period of significant change for England as the older structures of society that had been inherited from the medieval era began to give way to those that looked more like modern ones. There were changes in religion, politics, thought, and economics. There was even a change in the calendar.

Wesley lived through these changes and responded to many of them. How one sees Wesley relating to his culture, however, is still a matter of much debate. For a long time, many people—particularly Wesley's Methodist offspring—found it important to emphasize Wesley's life and work as a reaction *against* the "corrupting" trends of church and society in eighteenth-century Britain. So certain features of Wesley's time were emphasized—such as the decline in church attendance or the increasing numbers of urban poor—because these were the things to which Wesley most creatively responded. Other features of Wesley's response to his time, ones that showed his commonality with it—such as his opposition to the American Revolution or his refusal to officially withdraw from the Church of England—were given less weight.

In the last half-century or so, however, historians have changed the way they looked at the eighteenth century, and many Christians have renewed their commitment to focus on what unites various Christian groups instead of what divides them. Contemporary biographers of Wesley now tend to highlight those things Wesley had in common with his era and his "home church." On the basis of these commonalities, some Wesleyans even want to hold Wesley up as a resource to all of Christianity and not just as the champion and founder of Methodist Protestantism.

Both perspectives have their good and bad points, but beginning readers of Wesley ought to feel no pressure to take sides in such a debate. As with so many things about Wesley, it is better to take a both-and approach to Wesley's engagement with his context than an either-or one. Wesley was both a product of his time and a challenge to it. He was an exemplar of the "middle way" of Anglicanism and a thorn in its institutional side. He was a man who represented some of the ideals of his time, but he also reminded his hearers of the many ways in which English life fell far short of its own ideals.

Here then are a few crucial features of Wesley's context that provide helpful background for understanding his life and thought. Even though we can only scratch the surface of the deep issues involved, these features should be enough to give the reader who is unfamiliar with eighteenth-century England a basic sense of the time. Those features are the established and Protestant church of the country (the Church of England), the political turmoil of the day, the intellectual climate of the time, and the way in which society was changing. In each case, we will explain the issues involved and then foreshadow just a bit of how those issues are important for understanding Wesley.

The Established, Protestant Church of England

One good place to start putting together the pieces of Wesley's context is with the Church of England, which we today also refer to as the Anglican Church. This is the church that nurtured and ordained him and then had to wrestle with the challenges he presented and the issues he raised. Most people alive today, whether they agree with it or not, are familiar with the concept of a separation between church and state. Wesley's world, however, was not. The opinion of the great majority of the English during Wesley's lifetime was that church and state were two inseparable facets of society that were to work together for each other's mutual good.

Nearly two hundred years before Wesley's time, in 1534, King Henry VIII separated the Church of England from the "Church of Rome" and made himself the head of the church as well as the state. He believed, as did most people in Wesley's day, that he ruled by divine right, and so to disobey the king was ultimately to disobey God. In the king, church and state were thus indivisibly linked, but that link also permeated English society outside the palace. For example, bishops in the Church of England had seats in the House of Lords, the upper chamber of the English Parliament. This gave them political power but could also distract them from their pastoral duties. Many other government officials, such as justices of the peace, were also clergy, so people often engaged with the church and the state at the same time. Finally, there were laws that enforced Anglican belief and practice, so religion was always a legal matter and not just a moral or personal one.

All this made the Church of England the "established" church in English society, meaning that it was the only official religion of the country. Only those members of the Church of England who regularly took Communion could hold a political office. Though by Wesley's day there was official toleration for those who disagreed with the church's teachings or structure, toleration was not the same thing as freedom of religion. Dissenters or Nonconformists, as they were called, were usually not prosecuted for their disagreement, but their disagreement was still technically illegal. They were also subject to restrictions that were severe enough to make many of them unhappy with England's Anglican monarchy. Nevertheless, Henry VIII's union of church and state proved very durable and only began to break down at the end of Wesley's life.[1]

Knowing about this is important because Wesley always had an ambiguous relationship to his "mother church." On the one hand, he explicitly defended this "established church" system. Wesley affirmed that God was the basis of government, that kings ruled by divine right, and he used that idea to argue against the American Revolution. He resisted the idea of registering his Methodists as Dissenters, and he remained an Anglican priest to his dying day. On the other hand, Wesley often acted in ways that compromised this principle. He valued the mission of the church to save souls and make people holy more than he valued the Anglican structures that were supposed to support that mission. Wesley's use of lay preachers rather than officially ordained ones, his disregard for parish boundaries, and his ordaining of priests all challenged the established church from the inside just as Dissenters did from the outside. After the American Revolution, Wesley encouraged the American Methodists to function as a free and independent church that did not need government support. So while Wesley shared the basic assumption that church and state were connected, he was committed to an ideal of Christianity that made him challenge some parts of the church-state system and this got him into trouble. We will see many examples of this as we walk through Wesley's life.

Political Turmoil

England's political history in the eighteenth century—as well as the half-century or so leading up to it—was also connected to religious issues. These issues formed the background against which people discussed both religion and politics, and they even shaped England's international affairs and its place on the world stage.

England's political-religious upheaval began in the Reformation in the 1530s, but it reached a critical peak with the English Civil Wars of 1642-51 and the Puritan Commonwealth and Protectorate of 1649-59. The Puritans were those in the Church of England who wanted to "purify" it of liturgical elements and make it more like the Protestant churches of the European continent. Most people who lived through this turmoil had died by Wesley's time, but the cultural memory of those events still shaped English fears and concerns. Although there were serious economic issues that fed those civil wars, the popular understanding of them was as religious conflicts in which radical Protestants had killed the king, exiled his son, and then unsuccessfully tried to govern the country and impose their radical religion on everyone else.

To many Anglicans, these events proved how dangerous religious fanaticism could be. It was not just that people disagreed about doctrine and practice.

It was that people were so emotionally invested in their religion that they were willing to kill for their ideas. The memory of these conflicts with the Puritans made people suspicious of any emotional religion that deviated from a "normal" pattern of moral religion and moderate church attendance (whether at established Anglican churches or registered Nonconformist ones). Such religious fervor was not just distasteful; it might actually be a threat to the country.

This helps us understand why Wesley faced such serious opposition. It is one thing to have a few odd preachers who want people to be more religious than they are. It is quite another if stirring up religious emotions could be seen as a prelude to civil war. As we will see, in Wesley's lifetime, this took the form of both censure from society's elite and mob violence against the Methodists from those farther down on the social scale.

The conflict with the Puritans also shaped the theological environment of the Church of England, which was officially restored to its former position along with the restoration of the monarchy. Since the Puritans wanted to do away with "high church" things such as bishops and prayer books, the newly restored Anglican leaders naturally emphasized them. The Puritans were strong Calvinists in their theology, emphasizing the complete sinfulness of humanity and the doctrine of predestination. Therefore, it was easy for Anglican leaders to emphasize opposing ideas like the pursuit of holiness through good works and the means of grace or the idea that people were not predestined but had free will.

These anti-Puritan emphases were imposed on the church, and this forced many ministers (including both of Wesley's grandfathers) to resign their Church of England positions and become Dissenters. This attitude also pervaded the Church of England's minister training schools, such as Oxford, which Wesley attended as a young man. Wesley was, thus, exposed to both sides of this debate, and we shall see that his own attitudes were an eclectic mix of the positions represented by the Puritans and by the so-called Caroline Divines (since "Carol" is the Latin form of "Charles," the new king).

Things did not simply quiet down for England when the Convention Parliament of 1660 invited Charles II—the exiled son of the king whom an earlier Parliament had beheaded—to return from exile and occupy the English throne. Charles II had spent the intervening decade in exile in France, and this was suspicious for two reasons. First, France had been England's ancient "enemy," or at least their "sibling rival," for hundreds of years. Second, related to that, France was also staunchly Roman Catholic. This made it a religious adversary as well as a political one.

Charles II was supposed to be the head of the Church of England, a Protestant church, so any ties to Roman Catholicism were suspicious. These suspicions were confirmed when Charles joined the Roman Catholic Church on his deathbed. The problem became even worse under the reign of his brother, James II. James's strong pro-French and pro-Catholic leanings eventually led to a revolution. Seven English nobles invited James's Protestant daughter, Mary, and her Dutch husband, William of Orange, to invade the country and save the English throne for Protestantism. James fled back to France after a few minor skirmishes in an event remembered in Wesley's day as the Glorious Revolution of 1688. William and Mary were then recognized by Parliament as joint rulers, even though the previous king was still alive.

With this change in monarchy, two important political orientations arose in England, eventually coming together as political parties. One party, known as the Whigs, emphasized the role of the English Parliament in English government, and they sought to give that body an ever-increasing priority and control. The other party, known as Tories, felt that the king should be seen as the central element in government and that he was to be obeyed in all things.

The Glorious Revolution cast a long shadow over most of Wesley's life, even though it happened fifteen years before he was born. Most English had not taken sides during the invasion, either to defend their king or to aid his rival. When the dust settled, they accepted the new situation and took their oaths of loyalty to the new monarchs. A significant minority, however, could not accept this outcome. On principle, they believed that a monarch only ruled by divine right and that no group of people—nobles, Parliament, or otherwise—could change that. They could not swear oaths to their new king because they believed that James II was still their rightful king, however much they might disagree with his religion or his politics. These people were known as nonjurors (because they refused to swear the loyalty oath), and they were excluded from England's official political and religious life. As we shall see, Wesley's mother, Susanna, had sympathies in that direction, and that caused problems in the home.

Mary died in 1694, and William reigned alone as king until his death in 1702. He was followed on the throne by James's other Protestant daughter, Anne. By the time Queen Anne was crowned, James himself had passed away, so there were fewer principled objections to her becoming queen, but there were still some who believed that James's male heirs—particularly his son James and his grandson Charles—were still the rightful rulers of England. These people were called Jacobites (after the Hebrew and Greek forms of the name "James"), and armed Jacobite rebellions intent on putting the Old Pretender (James III) or the Young Pretender (Charles III) on the throne would unsettle England for the next fifty years or so.

Neither William and Mary nor Queen Anne and her husband had any surviving children. So to secure England's throne for Protestantism, Parliament assigned the royal succession to the granddaughter of a previous king (James I of England, who ruled from 1603 to 1625) and to her Protestant heirs. Queen Anne died in 1714, when Wesley was only eleven, and so George, Elector of Hanover in Germany, became George I of England. The very next year, 1715, there was a significant Jacobite uprising in northern England and Scotland, often known as the Fifteen. Another such uprising happened in 1745 (predictably known as the Forty-Five), near the beginning of Wesley's Evangelical Revival. Behind these uprisings, there was always the threat that the French would invade England and help restore James II's descendants to the throne and hence Roman Catholicism to England. It was not until Britain's military victories over France in the 1740s-60s and the coming of George III to the throne in 1760 that this threat subsided. It was, however, soon replaced by the looming threat of American independence.

Knowing this political background helps us to make sense of a couple of features of Wesley's writing and people's reaction to it. First of all, Wesley's era felt politically insecure, and Wesley often addressed that insecurity. Many of his works reflect a man addressing an unsettled time, and Wesley worked not only to calm unnecessary fears but also to use the insecurity of this world to point people toward the next one.

Second, this helps us see why Wesley was often accused of "popery," as Roman Catholicism was derisively called in Wesley's day, since such attacks could paint Wesley as both a political and a religious threat. In such an either-or political environment, Wesley's both-and arguments were often misunderstood and misinterpreted. Anything he said that sounded too much like Puritan or Roman Catholic theology would lead to attacks from Anglicans, since they were used to fighting on both of those fronts. Wesley, then, was caught in a triangle of theological concerns between Puritanism, Roman Catholicism, and the Church of England. Since Wesley often had to defend himself against very different—even opposite—attacks, some of his defenses sound confused, even contradictory. The better we understand this political-religious background, the better we will understand Wesley's response to it.

Intellectual Climate

Politics and religion were not the only things on the public stage of eighteenth-century English life, however dominant they may seem at times. Wesley's age was often styled the Age of Reason, and there were many intellectual changes happening, particularly in science and philosophy. Sometimes Wesley approved of these new ideas, but other times he opposed them. While Wesley admired reason, philosophy, and science, he also saw their limits, and this tension is important for the way he thought.

Science as a discipline grew in importance and visibility in English culture during Wesley's life. People pursued scientific knowledge and began to adopt a scientific outlook on the world. Soon after the Restoration, King Charles II founded the Royal Society of London for the Improving of Natural Knowledge (more commonly known simply as the Royal Society). This gave an official, royal backing to the advance of scientific knowledge and a public stamp of approval on scientific projects. Famous Royal Society presidents, such as Isaac Newton (1643–1727), focused more public attention on science. Scientific inventions, particularly ones involving textile technology and steam power, set up England to become the first industrialized country, and science became an acceptable—sometimes even expected—pursuit of the leisure classes.

The antagonism many today feel between science and religion had not yet developed in Wesley's day. Many of England's noted scientists, such as Isaac Newton and Joseph Priestley, had strong religious interests and inclinations (though admittedly not always toward the traditional doctrines of Christianity). Most people saw science as perfectly compatible with—even a natural consequence of—a belief in a Creator God. Not only did most scientists believe in God, but also a number of prominent bishops of the Church of England spoke of science with high praise, and clergy were often engaged in scientific pursuits themselves.

Wesley was very much a man of his time when it comes to this issue. He had a strong interest in science and enjoyed reading about the new inventions and discoveries—particularly those that promised to improve people's lives. Wesley himself wrote on electricity and compiled a very popular list of home remedies called *Primitive Physick*, which he insisted was based on empirical observation.[2] He urged the study of science in the school that he founded in Kingswood, among his Methodist preachers, and even to all ministers, claiming that it was important for understanding the Bible.[3] Wesley saw science, then, as an aid to faith and not a threat.

However, the philosophy that arose alongside of science was another matter completely. Where science was practical and gave people a good way to understand the physical world, Wesley agreed with it and used it. He was even somewhat scientific in his approach to religious concerns. But when science offered a naturalistic worldview with no room for divine intervention, Wesley opposed it with all his might. Alongside Wesley's interest in science, we also find him believing in ghosts and witches. He argued for the limitations of scientific knowledge and for a divine providence that worked alongside the physical causes of things. So while science was important to Wesley, its philosophy did not govern his world. This attitude comes through in many of his works throughout his life.

Changes in Society

Along with these changes in thought, changes in patterns of living arose in the eighteenth century as well. Most of these changes were gradual but clear. Slowly but surely, the social landscape of England changed as commerce developed and cities and towns became more important. Wesley found in these changes many opportunities for ministry that were being missed by the more traditional established church.

Many significant changes were economic ones introduced by advances in technology and new opportunities for trade. For most of its history, England was a rural society whose primary economic activity was farming and raising livestock, to which was added a host of cottage industries such as making cloth. It had only one city of any significant size, London, and most of its citizens lived in the country rather than in town. Towns were mainly places for tradesmen to gather to sell goods and for the upper classes to gather for social events. This slowly changed during Wesley's life.

New modes of production encouraged people to live closer together for economic reasons. People began to move to the towns to find employment, but that meant leaving the family-and-village support networks that had held up English society for so long. The loss of these networks left people vulnerable both to the accidents of life and to the temptations of anonymous urban living. The established church had a difficult time keeping up with these changes, and so fewer and fewer people were being effectively served by its parish system and the structure for pastoral ministry that it dictated. Church attendance declined during this period, and most people thought morality did as well.

Whether one reads Wesley's activity as a supplement to the church or as a challenge to it, his most distinctive practices arise from this changing social background. Class meetings and field preaching addressed spiritual needs left unmet by traditional church structures. The Methodist movement thrived in towns where Church of England structures were lacking, as well as in those rural areas where the same was true. Even Wesley's work in compassionate ministry—such as founding dispensaries for the poor or starting a school for coal miners' children—is best understood as a response to the increasing ineffectiveness of the traditional means of social support.

One final change was not so significant for Wesley's time, but it certainly affects the way we today read about it. Halfway through Wesley's life, England changed calendars, creating two separate systems of recording the dates of events. The old calendar, called the Julian calendar, had been in use since the Roman Empire. According to that calendar, each year contained exactly $365\frac{1}{4}$ days. The problem was that this formula was about eleven minutes off, which made the calendar year lag behind the solar year (as reckoned by equinoxes and solstices). For Catholic countries, Pope Gregory XIII fixed this problem in 1582 with his Gregorian calendar, which was more accurate and which closed the gap between the solar year and the calendar year. Protestant England originally did not want to follow this Catholic idea, but by the 1750s it had become a problem. So they adopted the new calendar and reset their dates to match everyone else's. So, for example, when Wesley was born, calendars in England said it was June 17, 1703. After 1752, however, Wesley celebrated his birthday on June 28, which was the date the Gregorian calendar would have said had it been used at the time. At the same time, England also moved the start of the New Year officially back to January 1 (the legal year used to begin on March 25), which explains why many dates in Wesley's letters are written with two dates (e.g., February 1740/41). When that happens, it is the second year that conforms to our modern way of numbering.

There is much more that could be said about the times in which Wesley lived and served, but this is sufficient to orient us for now. With this bit of background, we will be more alert to some of the important features of Wesley's context and have more tools to make sense of his life. And so it is to that life that we must now turn.

two
Family Background and Early Life
(1600s–1720)

---

*W*hen exploring someone's life, it is hard to start "at the beginning" because "the beginning" is difficult to define. We could start with a birth, but even that important event occurs "in the middle of things," surrounded by influences and factors that will have a profound effect on how that young life will develop. Though there is much to learn from looking deep into the Wesley family's past, we will start with a simple sketch of John Wesley's parents' lives before he was born.[1] We will then move on through a few episodes of his early life that he or his parents found significant enough to write down, and we will finish with our young Wesley ready to enter Oxford University.

John Wesley was raised in a family that embodied many of the religious concerns that we touched on in the last chapter. His parents were both highly principled individuals who had returned to the Anglican Church after having been raised in strong dissenting families. Thus, both of them exposed their children to the rich devotional traditions of the Nonconformists and Puritans and also to the high church principles that had lured each of them back separately to full communion with the Church of England.

John Wesley's mother was born Susanna Annesley, the daughter of Samuel Annesley (1620-96), the leader of the Dissenters in London. Rev. Annesley had been removed from his position as pastor of St. Giles, Cripplegate, in London in 1662, back when the Church of England was purging Puritan influence from its ranks in the aftermath of those civil wars we discussed in the previous chapter. Susanna was his twenty-fifth and final child (though most of her siblings had died in infancy), and she was born on January 20, 1669. Apparently, Susanna's father passed on to his daughter more a capacity for strong conviction than he did the content of those convictions, however. About the age of thirteen—after unusually precocious research and deliberation—Susanna abandoned the dissenting tradition of her parents and began attending Anglican services on her own. Whatever Samuel Annesley's private feelings were about Susanna's dissent from his dissenting tradition, he gave his daughter his blessing and remained very close to her until the end of his life.

This habit of reflection and deliberation was to characterize Susanna throughout her life. She only published one thing during her lifetime, an anonymous open letter defending her son, but she also wrote many pastoral and theological letters to her children and kept a self-reflective journal. In her collected works,[2] we can see that she was a careful thinker and that she knew well the philosophical and theological issues of the day. Wesley's different interpreters have different opinions about the exact ways in which his mother influenced him, but the fact of her influence on his theological foundation is hard to deny.

Shortly after the young Susanna cast her lot with the established church, she attended the wedding of her elder sister Elizabeth. There she met another young (though still six years her senior) "dissenting dissenter" named Samuel Wesley. Like Susanna, Samuel's father, John Wesley (our Wesley's namesake), had been removed from his parish in 1662, just before Samuel was born. Unlike Susanna's father, who had inherited sufficient means from his family to provide for himself when he lost his job as a pastor, Samuel's father was thrown into poverty and died of hardship when Samuel was only eight years old. Through the generosity of others, Samuel was educated at a number of dissenting schools until the age of twenty-one. Then, as he was trying to answer some of the Anglican critiques against his dissenting tradition, Samuel found himself convinced by them and rejoined the Church of England instead. He and Susanna kept up their friendship and correspondence, likely fired by their similar trajectories, and the two of them were married on November 12, 1688, even as William of Orange was making his march through England in the events that were to culminate in the Glorious Revolution.

It took Samuel nearly three years to secure his first full-time pastorate, and he spent the time as an interim pastor, as a navy chaplain, and as a freelance writer. John Wesley's brother Samuel was born during these years of financial hardship, and they foreshadowed the money troubles that would follow the older Wesleys throughout their lives. Finally, in 1691, the Wesleys moved to a very rural parish in South Ormsby, Lincolnshire. Life was still difficult there (Susanna gave birth to six children while at South Ormsby, but only three survived infancy), but the family struggled through until Samuel was forced to resign the parish because he had confronted the mistress of the local landlord. It was this highly principled but costly act that precipitated the family's move, around 1697, to the parish at Epworth, where Samuel was to serve for the rest of his life.

Samuel's start at Epworth was difficult, but his careful attention to his pastoral duties eventually won most of the community over. Still, the family struggled financially. Most of the children born during that time died, their barn collapsed, and there was a fire in part of the rectory (or parsonage). Samuel, however, stayed attentive to his ministry and also worked on an academic project that would become his life's work: a detailed commentary on the book of Job. Then, in late 1701, Rev. Wesley again displayed his costly devotion to principle, this time in a way that clashed with the equally strong principles of his wife.

Samuel believed in the divine right of kings, but he also believed that King William's invasion during the Glorious Revolution was necessary for preserving Protestantism (and hence his chosen church) in England. Susanna, however, did not share this opinion. John Wesley described the conflict to a friend in this way: "'Sukey,' said my father to my mother, one day, after family prayer, 'why did you not say amen this morning to the prayer for the king?' 'Because,' said she, 'I do not believe the *prince of Orange* to be king.' 'If that be the case,' said he, 'you and I must part; for if we have *two* kings, we must have *two beds*.'"[3] At that point, Samuel Wesley headed off to London and did not return for the rest of the year. Fortunately for the harmony of the Wesley family, King William died in March of 1702, and both Samuel and Susanna could agree on his successor, Queen Anne. Neither party backed down, but the conflict was over. A little over a year later, on June 17, 1703,[4] John Wesley—called Jacky by most of his family—was born.

Much later in his life, John Wesley requested of his mother her rules for raising her children. Susanna's reflections provide an interesting glimpse into what life must have been like for the family of the Epworth rectory. Her methods were highly disciplined with strict schedules for eating and playing, but these reflected her own character.[5] Misbehavior was strictly punished, but obedience was frequently rewarded. Most of this discipline was geared toward the children's religious education, which Susanna felt to be her most important duty. "I insist upon conquering the will of children betimes [early], because this is the only strong and rational foundation of a religious education," she wrote to her son.[6] An emphasis on self-control was extended to even the ordinary behavior of children. For example, children were taught to cry quietly, so "that most odious noise of the crying of children was rarely heard in the house; but the family usually lived in as much quietness as if there had not been a child among them."[7] Susanna also saw to the rest of the children's education (though even here, when she taught them to read, it was from the Bible). She especially insisted, unusually for that age, that the girls learn to read before learning any of the other "womanly work" that society wanted them to do, such as sewing.

Perhaps Susanna's high sense of order in the family helped protect them somewhat from the chaos that always seemed to be threatening them. Some of this chaos was caused by Samuel's inability to handle money well, and so he was often in debt. In 1705, when Wesley was only two, there was a contentious political election in which Samuel's political views caused some trouble. In retaliation, one of his parishioners called in a debt that Samuel could not pay, and he was thrown into prison. There Samuel worked to pastor his fellow prisoners, trusting his wife to take care of his family. Fortunately, the elder Wesley's archbishop, John Sharpe, came to his rescue and, with assistance from some of Samuel's pastoral colleagues, paid off the debts that were keeping him in prison. During Samuel's imprisonment, the caring archbishop visited Susanna and her family and asked her about how well she was doing, whether or not she ever "wanted bread." Her response seems emblematic of the financial conditions of the Wesley home. "My Lord," she responded, "I will freely own to your Grace, that strictly speaking, I never did want bread. But then, I have had so much care to get it before 'twas eat[en], and to pay for it after, as has often made it very unpleasant to me. And I think to have bread on such terms is the next degree of wretchedness to having none at all."[8]

John Wesley would have been too young to remember well the incident of his father's imprisonment, but there was another misfortune that he remembered very well indeed. It may have even played some role in the development of his sense of calling. On the night of February 9, 1709, a fire started in the Epworth rectory, likely from some sparks hitting the dry roof. Fire falling on her bed awakened one of John's sisters, Hetty, and she called out an alarm. Samuel Wesley heard people outside calling "Fire!" and awoke to find it was his own house that was ablaze.

As one could imagine, a good deal of confusion followed. Samuel woke his pregnant wife, who woke the maid, who gathered the youngest infant in her arms and bade the other children in the nursery to wake and follow her. With the help of his oldest daughters, Samuel managed to get most of his family out of the front door even through the flames. Other children escaped to the street through windows, but when Samuel tried to return to the house to make sure everyone was safe, the stairs collapsed under his weight. Back outside, they realized they had all the children except little Jacky. Here is Wesley's account, written much later, of what happened next:

I believe it was just at that time I waked; for I did not cry, as they imagined, unless it was afterward. I remember all the circumstances as distinctly as though it were but yesterday. Seeing the room was very light, I called to the maid to take me up. But none answering, I put my head out of the curtains and saw streaks of fire on the top of the room. . . . I then climbed up on a chest which stood near the window: one in the yard saw me, and proposed running to fetch a ladder. Another answered, "There will not be time; but I have thought of another expedient: here I will fix myself against the wall; lift a light man, and set him on my shoulders." They did so, and he took me out of the window. Just then the whole roof fell in; but it fell inward, or we had all been crushed at once. When they brought me into the house, where my father was, he cried out, "Come, neighbours! Let us kneel down! Let us give thanks to God! He has given me all my eight children: let the house go; I am rich enough!"[9]

Just how much this remarkable rescue influenced Wesley is a matter of debate. Susanna later wrote in her meditation journal, "I do intend to be more particularly careful of the soul of this child that thou has so mercifully provided for."[10] Later, Wesley referred to himself using (admittedly out of context) the biblical phrase "a brand plucked from the burning" (see Zech. 3:2). This phrase became a kind of emblem for Wesley, and he identified with it and used it on an epitaph he composed for himself when he thought he was dying. While he would later deny that this gave him any sense of a special calling or destiny, it would nevertheless stick in his memory.

The fire destroyed all the Wesleys' family possessions, and it forced them to live apart, farmed out to various houses in the village until the house could be rebuilt. But the strong leadership of both father and mother kept the family together in spite of hardship. While Samuel did his part, it was Susanna who was mostly responsible for family cohesion. Even when Samuel was away, she did whatever she needed to (as she did when he was in prison) to care for the family's physical and spiritual needs, even when her actions created conflict.

In 1711, Samuel Wesley was again away from home, this time to London as an official representative to the Convocation, the official governing body of the Church of England. His assistant, Rev. Inman, however, would only conduct one service on Sundays, and he seemed to only preach about the obligation of Christians to pay their debts. Since everyone knew that Samuel was frequently in debt, there was little secret about the target of those attacks.

Since spiritual care was clearly lacking, Susanna decided to hold Sunday evening services for her family in her home. They would sing, read Scripture, and Susanna would read a sermon from one of Samuel's books. First the servants wanted to join, and then some of the neighbors. Before long, Susanna had more people in her home on Sunday evening than were at church on Sunday morning, perhaps as many as three hundred. The assistant complained to Samuel in London, calling the services "conventicles," a word that referred to illegal and seditious meetings of Dissenters. In response, Samuel wrote back to his wife, asking her to stop her meetings, even though he had known about them for a while from Susanna's own letters.

Susanna's replies to her husband reveal her spiritual concerns and the force of her personality. In her first reply, she explained why she started the services and answered his objection about a woman conducting church services. In her second reply, she detailed all the good that was being done by the services. She was getting a lot of people back to church that had not been there for a while, and her work was building goodwill between the Wesley family and their parishioners. She finished that reply with these remarkable words:

If you do after all think fit to dissolve this assembly, do not tell me any more that you desire me to do it, for that will not satisfy my conscience; but send your positive command in such full and express terms as may absolve me from all guilt and punishment for neglecting this opportunity of doing good to souls, when you and I shall appear before the great and awful tribunal of our Lord Jesus Christ.

I dare not wish this practice of ours had never been begun, but it will be with extreme [?] grief that I shall dismiss them, because I foresee the consequences. I pray God direct and bless you.[11]

There was no more discussion after that. The services continued until Samuel got home. After that, the family always held a higher place in the community's esteem.

This was the strong spiritual and principled environment that Wesley left when, at the age of ten, he was sent off to be educated at Charterhouse school in London, an opportunity he received at the nomination of the Duke of Buckingham. It was a typical English school in many respects, with a tradition of strict discipline from the teachers and of mistreatment from the older students. Charterhouse was Wesley's home for the next six years. Although he received a strong education that enabled him to move on to Oxford University, Wesley later remembered the time more for the lessening of the spiritual fervor that had been given him by his parents. Wesley recalled, "The next six or seven years were spent at school; where, outward restraints being removed, I was much more negligent than before even of outward duties, and almost continually guilty of outward sins, which I knew to be such, though they were not scandalous in the eye of the world. However, I still read the Scriptures, and said my prayers, morning and evening."[12]

As we can see, Wesley was still religious, though less so than he was at home. His behavior was probably quite exemplary, and we know that he was a favorite of the schoolmaster Thomas Walker. But he did not yet have the seriousness that would mark out the rest of his life. That came during his time at Oxford, where Wesley went in 1720.

three

Oxford and the Holy Club
(1720-35)

---

*W*esley's admission to Oxford University began an academic career that would occupy him for the next fifteen years. These were important and formative years for Wesley, imprinting a scholastic stamp on his character that would endure throughout his life. During these years he became a minister in the Church of England and adopted the reading and writing habits that would produce his tremendous literary legacy. He also began his own pursuit and teaching of holiness, which would end up being his most important theological contribution to the church. Once again, we cannot do justice to all of the events of, and influences on, Wesley's life during this time, and so we must content ourselves with a small and representative sample.[1]

Wesley arrived in Oxford shortly after his seventeenth birthday in the summer of 1720. There, he had been admitted to Christ Church College, a college already known for such notable graduates as the philosopher John Locke and the American colonialist William Penn. The college also had strong ties to the Church of England. Originally founded by Cardinal Thomas Wolsey as Cardinal's College before the English Reformation, the college was refounded by Henry VIII in 1546 and made the home of the bishop for the newly created diocese of Oxford.

For the next four years, Christ Church would be Wesley's home, with occasional time spent with his elder brother in London and, less frequently, back with his father and mother in Epworth. As a graduate of Charterhouse school, he was entitled to a small stipend, but his undergraduate years were still lean ones for the young scholar. Like his father, he was often in debt. Nevertheless, he seems to have enjoyed his undergraduate days to the full. He was known to take part in many of the sports available (such as rowing, riding, and tennis), he attended coffee shops, occasionally the theater, and he had many friends.

College was more than social life to Wesley, however. He also pursued his academic work with dedication and energy, at first reading whatever interested him but eventually settling into a strict pattern of studies. He focused on the classics and took a keen interest in logic, which he mastered rather well and which would become a feature of his discourse for the rest of his life. Literary critic Samuel Badcock, on the basis of letters he had read from the time and conversations with Wesley's family, described the young John Wesley in this way: "[He was] the very sensible and acute collegian baffling every man by the subtleties of logic, and laughing at them for being so easily routed; a young fellow of the finest classical taste, of the most liberal and manly sentiments . . . gay and sprightly, with a turn for wit and humour."[2]

Wesley finished his undergraduate work in 1724 and decided to stay in Oxford to pursue his master's degree. In September of that year, Susanna raised the issue with her son of entering the ministry as a profession. Susanna's reason was that she wanted John to come and help his father as a curate and so be nearer to the family. Wesley warmed to the idea, and in January 1725 he mentioned the idea in a letter to his father. Samuel Wesley approved, though he cautioned his son to make such a move only for the best reasons. Susanna was more enthusiastic and hoped that Wesley could be ordained as a deacon by summer. In giving advice on how to prepare, Samuel urged academic study, particularly of the Bible and its original languages, but Susanna emphasized reading in more practical areas ("'Tis an unhappiness almost peculiar to our family," Susanna wrote to her son, "that your father and I seldom think alike"[3]). There was, however, soon common agreement between the parents that entering the ministry would help Wesley in his own spiritual development, and along with Wesley, they agreed that this was the course to pursue.

As Wesley settled into the idea of ministry, another opportunity began to present itself. In May 1725, there was a resignation among the group of fellows of Lincoln College, also there at Oxford. In the Oxford University system, the fellows of a college—in Lincoln's case there were twelve—were the tutors and lecturers who formed the official governing body of that college. They were given a place to live at the college, freedom to pursue their academic work, and even a small stipend, which they could supplement by taking on their own students. These were highly prized positions, and this particular one required its holder to have been born in the diocese of Lincoln. As that was where Epworth was conveniently located, Wesley decided to apply for the slot, and his father helped with his recommendations.

As Wesley was preparing for his ordination and hoping to secure his fellowship, Wesley encountered two works that were to have a strong impact on his spiritual development. He corresponded with his mother over them, thought through them carefully, and would later recommend them to others throughout his life. The first was a pair of books, sometimes printed together, by Jeremy Taylor called *Rules and Exercises of Holy Living* and *Rules and Exercises of Holy Dying*. He had been advised by a friend not to read it until he was older, but he read it anyway, and it caused him to consecrate his life entirely to God. "Instantly," Wesley wrote as he reflected on the impact of the work on his life, "I resolved to dedicate *all my life* to God; *all* my thoughts, and words, and actions; being thoroughly convinced, there was no medium, but that *every part* of my life (not *some* only) must either be a sacrifice to God or to myself, that is, in effect, to the devil."[4]

The second book was *The Imitation of Christ*, or *The Christian's Pattern*, usually attributed to Thomas à Kempis. He might have even read this book before Taylor's, having discussed some of the issues it raises in a letter to his mother in May of 1725, but the later Wesley dates its effectiveness in his life to the following year. In any case, while Wesley disagreed with the book on a number of issues—especially the idea that God seemed to want people to be miserable in this life—the book's ideas about how a soul was to seek communion with God resonated with the ideas from Taylor's work. Later Wesley wrote, "I met with Kempis's *Christian Pattern*. The nature and extent of *inward religion*, the religion of the heart, now appeared to me in a stronger light than ever it had done before."[5] This would be a book that Wesley himself would republish, and he recommended it throughout his life.

Wesley's biographers often differ on how to interpret the strong spiritual orientation these books helped to produce. Some, following Wesley's own mature interpretation, see this dedication as the true root of his spirituality. Others focus on the idea that this orientation (as demonstrated by the events that followed) still contained a strong element of working for his salvation. These writers usually hold off an "evangelical conversion" for Wesley until later (typically 1738). However one interprets these events, they show Wesley to be a spiritually serious twenty-two-year-old, and they also set the stage for the events that will follow.

The next eighteen months of Wesley's life were marked by numerous successes. He was ordained a deacon on September 19, 1725, and continued his studies at Oxford through that next year. After sitting for an examination in Greek and Latin classics, Wesley was duly elected a fellow of Lincoln College on March 17, 1726, and his brother Charles joined him at Oxford (enrolling in Christ Church) in May. Later that year, in November, Wesley's recognized mastery of Greek and logic led to his election both as a lecturer in Greek and as the moderator of the daily debates, called disputations, at the college. Finally, on February 14, 1727, Wesley was awarded his master of arts degree.

Although things were going well for Wesley's career, there were at the same time stresses in the Wesley home, many of them revolving around his older sister Mehetabel, whom everyone called Hetty. In May 1725, Hetty had eloped with a lover whose identity is unknown but who immediately betrayed and left her. Disgraced and most likely pregnant, she had tried to return home, but Wesley's father would have none of it. To cover her shameful pregnancy, she married that October, had the baby shortly before Wesley's election as fellow, but then lost the child by the end of the year. Some of Hetty's siblings, including John, had tried to stand up for her, while others, like the eldest, Samuel Jr., had taken her father's side. This caused considerable strain in the family and a few cold letter exchanges, but eventually things thawed. They were sufficiently patched by August of 1727 for Wesley to leave Oxford and finally answer his mother's wish to help his father in ministry.

Wesley stayed in Lincolnshire, helping his father at the parishes of Epworth and Wroot (which his father had also been given in 1722), from August 1727 until October 1729. He preached every week at one of these two parishes, performed his pastoral duties, and continued to read spiritual works. These years were not, apparently, very fulfilling to Wesley, and he did not seem to enjoy parish ministry as much as he enjoyed his academic life at Oxford. He returned to Oxford for a few months in 1728 to prepare for and receive his full ordination as a priest, which happened on September 22 of that year, but then he dutifully returned to Epworth. A year later, however, he was summoned back to Lincoln College by the rector, Dr. John Morley, who insisted that the terms of his fellowship required that he fulfill his duties in person. And so, in November 1729, Wesley was back in Oxford, where he was to remain for the next six years.

While Wesley was away at Epworth, his brother Charles had begun meeting with another young man named William Morgan, and perhaps one or two others, for times of prayer and study. John had visited this group back in May of 1729, but the group had broken up over that summer when Charles joined John in Epworth, and Morgan returned home. Once John returned, however, the group reassembled, eventually joined by others, and it was this group that was first given the label "Methodists."

There is some debate over the origin of the epithet "Methodist." The group was originally taunted with labels such as the "Holy Club" or "Bible Moths," mocking them for their unusual seriousness about religion. Charles Wesley claims the group was called Methodists before John returned from Epworth. John remembers the name arising a few years later. There is also debate about what it meant, whether it came from their methodical approach to religion, from their keeping the methods of the university, or as a term of abuse first given to another fringe group and then reapplied to the Holy Club. However and whenever it came up, the name "Methodist" stuck, and this was how Wesley's followers would be known to history.

Wesley led this small group for the next six years. They devoted themselves to weekly Communion, to charitable works (visiting those in prison and giving to the poor), and above all to the study of Scripture. Their main resolve, Wesley was later to recount, was to be "Bible Christians." To a few people, the group's rigor was cause for admiration. One of those was George Whitefield, who had heard about the group even before he arrived at Oxford and earnestly sought an opportunity to join them. But to most, Wesley's approach to religion seemed harsh or extreme. Wesley, of course, felt that it was simply the approach dictated by the Scripture itself. "I have been charged," he noted in 1731 in a letter to a friend, "with being too strict, with carrying things too far in religion, and laying burdens on myself, if not on others, which were neither necessary nor possible to be borne. . . . To carry duties too far! Why, what is this but to change holiness itself into extravagance!"[6]

Accusations against Wesley came to a head in August of 1732 with the death of one of the original members of the Holy Club, William Morgan, who had been ailing both physically and mentally for nearly a year. Word spread around Oxford that Morgan had died from excessive fasting and that Wesley was to blame. As soon as Wesley heard these accusations, he preemptively wrote to William's father. That letter, which outlines the brief history and purposes of the Holy Club, was later reprinted and became the early standard justification for the movement. The letter satisfied William's father well enough for him to entrust his other son to Wesley's care, but he, too, eventually decided that Wesley's standards were unreasonable and harmful.

Despite these very high standards, it would be a mistake to view Wesley as a heartless religious machine, and this can be seen in his letters to the various women in his life to whom he turned for support. He wrote frequently to his mother and actively sought her advice. He also shared in a letter writing circle with a number of married women, some of them his age, some older. His letters to them over these years give the reader a picture of Wesley at odds with the strict disciplinarian he was seen to be at Oxford. They are pastoral and affectionate (too much so for his mother's sensibilities, in fact), and he comes across as that dashing young man of the early 1700s who many in his time would have aspired to be. Here, again, we see Wesley as a representative of his age even at the same time that he was trying to rise above it.

One thing unusual about Wesley was his emphasis on inward religion. "I take religion," he states in one of his letters, "to be, not the bare saying over so many prayers . . . not anything superadded now and then to a careless or worldly life; but a constant ruling habit of soul; a renewal of our minds in the image of God; a recovery of the divine likeness."[7] One of his earliest sermons along these lines was "Circumcision of the Heart," which he preached in 1733. Even after his famous Aldersgate experience (covered in the next chapter), Wesley would affirm that this was the best sermon he'd ever written on the topic.[8] Its mixed reception shows that there were many who approved of his evangelical approach as well as those who opposed it. It also demonstrates that Wesley's intellectual commitment to "heart religion" was in place long before Aldersgate gave his feelings the chance to catch up.

Back in Epworth, the elder Samuel Wesley's health was failing. He had never fully recovered from a disastrous fall from his wagon in 1731,[9] and now he sensed the end coming. His first concern was for his wife and the ministry in his parish after he died. He seemed to want to build a legacy there, and when he could not convince his oldest son and namesake to take his place, he began to press John to do so. John, however, was completely resistant. It is unclear whether his resistance came from his less-than-happy experience in the parish years earlier or—as he repeated to his father and brother in several letters over this time—from Wesley's belief that he could do more good, both for himself and for others, in Oxford. Samuel was insistent, but John equally so. That was where matters stood when John and Charles Wesley traveled to Epworth to be with their dying father on April 4, 1735.

We do not know what transpired in the meantime to change John's mind, but after his father's death on April 25, Wesley did apply for his father's position at Epworth. He was, however, too late, and it was assigned to someone else. John stayed in Epworth to help take care of the parish until he had the chance to go to London to present his father's magnum opus, his commentary on the book of Job, to the queen. There his life took a decidedly unexpected turn.

four
Georgia, Aldersgate, and the Start of Revival
(1735-39)

----

*W*esley stayed in Epworth for two months after his father's death, where he minded the parish until he saw he would not be named his father's replacement. He and Charles then traveled to London to make a formal presentation of Samuel Wesley's monumental work on the book of Job to the wife of King George II, Queen Caroline, to whom it was dedicated. While in London, Wesley was approached by several people—among them Governor James Oglethorpe—about the possibility of taking the missionary parish in Savannah, Georgia, in place of the one denied him in Epworth. The previous year, Samuel Wesley had recommended one of his sons-in-law for such a position, but Wesley only mentions hearing about it in August of 1735.

The colony of Georgia had been established in 1732 by James Oglethorpe as an answer to England's crowded and mismanaged debtors' prisons. The colony would give debtors an opportunity to work off their debts, and it would also form a buffer between the other English colonies to the north and the growing Spanish ones in Florida. Wesley was offered the chance to minister to the colonists there and to spread the gospel to the Native Americans with whom the colonists had come in contact.

Wesley thought about the offer for a month and decided that it would be for the best. For whatever reason, Samuel Wesley's death had created a decisive break between Wesley and Oxford, and he preferred this new opportunity to the idea of returning to his academic duties there. Charles Wesley decided to join his brother in this venture, and the two of them, with a few others, boarded the *Simmonds* on October 14, 1735, to head to Georgia.

Wesley's Time in Georgia

The trip to Georgia reveals much about the state of Wesley's mind and heart during this period of his life. On the one hand, he took it upon himself to minister to those on the ship, even studying German to better serve a group of Moravian immigrants who were also on board.[1] Wesley and his companions spent their time, as they had at Oxford, studying Scripture and devotional works, engaging the spiritual disciplines, and pastoring and preaching to their fellow shipmates.

These ministerial and academic pursuits, however, still left Wesley unsettled. Several times during the voyage, the *Simmonds* encountered fierce storms and waves. At one point, they were sure they were going to be sunk. Wesley found himself terrified of the idea of dying, which revealed the weakness of his faith and made him ashamed. The Moravian immigrants, on the other hand, seemed ready to meet their deaths with calm assurance, even holding church services in the midst of the storm. Wesley had never encountered such personally assured faith, and he noted in his *Journal*, upon seeing their behavior, that "this was the most glorious day which I have ever hitherto seen."[2]

The journey to Georgia took several months, and they finally arrived on February 5, 1736. One month later, Wesley began his ministry in Savannah. His first sermon was well attended, and the people seemed engaged, but as Wesley reflected later in his *Journal*, it was not a sign of things to come. In his own words, "I could hardly believe that the greater, the far greater part of this attentive, serious people, would hereafter trample under foot that Word, and say all manner of evil falsely of him that spake it."[3] Some of Wesley's difficulties were due, no doubt, to the rough nature of the first settlers of a debtors' colony, but Wesley did not help matters by the strict way he went about his ministry. The level of seriousness with which he took his responsibility was not matched by the level of seriousness with which people accepted it, and his liturgical ways did not fit well with the looser intuitions of the people. Once he even refused to baptize a young woman's child because she refused to do it the proper Anglican way.[4]

This disconnect was felt on both sides. Just three months into his ministry in Georgia, one of his parishioners, William Horton, freely told him, "I like nothing you do. All your sermons are satires on particular persons. Therefore I will never hear you more. And all the people are of my mind. . . . Indeed, there is neither man nor woman in the town who minds a word you say."[5] With such ringing endorsements, it is no wonder that Wesley's ministry in Georgia was short lived. However, Wesley might have been able to endure these frictions had his relationships with all of his parishioners not been disrupted by his relationship to just one of them, a young lady named Sophy Hopkey.

Wesley's relationship with Miss Hopkey is never mentioned in his published *Journal*, but it fills his private diaries. Though she was younger than Wesley by fifteen years and deeply connected to Savannah's elite, the two developed a romantic attachment, which seems to have begun with Sophy taking care of Wesley during an illness in August of 1736.[6] Wesley, however, could not seem to reconcile himself to the tension between the devotion to a woman and devotion to God. In early March of 1737, Wesley tried to settle the matter by lot, and the lot drawn said, "Think of it no more." Wesley claimed to feel a release on this, but it still shocked him when, a few days later, Sophy announced her engagement to one William Williamson, whom she married in less than a week.

After this, things began to fall apart quickly for Wesley. Over the next few months, he found numerous faults in the new Mrs. Williamson's religious behavior, which culminated in his public humiliation of her by barring her from Communion on August 7, 1737. Rumors began flying about Wesley, and soon a grand jury was assembled to look into the matter.

Over the next few months, Wesley came to see that there was little he could do to redeem his reputation, that his effective ministry in Savannah was over, and that even his original dream of ministering to the Native Americans was out of reach. When orders to detain him were circulated on December 2, he slipped away under the cover of dark and, in his words, "shook off the dust of my feet and left Georgia, after having preached the gospel (not as I ought, but as I was able) one year and nearly nine months."[7] Wesley made his way about forty miles north by foot, nearly getting lost in the swamps and woods several times, before reaching Port Royal, South Carolina. From there, he traveled by boat to Charleston, where he set sail for England on December 24, 1737.

Wesley's journey home gave him ample time for reflection, and he focused on his own spiritual inadequacy. Even while he was serving as the ship's pastor, his thoughts turned to his own need for spiritual direction. He felt convicted over his own level of unbelief, pride, and religious inattention, and he yearned for a faith much deeper than the one he had thus far possessed. "I went to America to convert the Indians," he wrote in his *Journal*, "but Oh! who shall convert me?"[8]

Aldersgate

Wesley arrived back in England on January 29, 1738, the prevailing winds making the journey east across the Atlantic much quicker than the journey west. He traveled to London to visit friends and relations and give a report to the trustees for the Georgia colony. There, about a week after his arrival, he met a young Moravian named Peter Böhler, who was to have a decisive influence on Wesley's spiritual development.

What Wesley felt to be at issue was the nature of saving faith. He had knowledge about God, he followed God's laws rather strictly, and he did all those things that he thought would please God, like giving to the poor and visiting the sick. But he lacked a clear assurance of his salvation, an intuitive sense that he trusted God and that God had accepted him. In Wesley's words, "The faith I want is, 'a sure trust and confidence in God, that through the merits of Christ my sins are forgiven, and I reconciled to the favour of God.'"[9] Wesley had seen glimpses of this in the other Moravians he had met, but it was Peter Böhler who was to introduce it to Wesley personally.

Over the next couple of months, Wesley made various journeys to see friends and relatives, preaching wherever he went and focusing on those themes with which he himself was struggling. Through many conversations, Peter Böhler told him that salvation came from faith alone and encouraged both Wesley brothers, John and Charles, to seek such faith. Wesley resisted the idea at first. However, after a careful reading of the Bible and after hearing from some witnesses that Peter Böhler had brought to him, all of whom testified about the reality of this faith in their own lives, he came to believe it and dedicated himself to seeking it.

As part of this search, John Wesley worked with Peter Böhler to start a small religious society in Fetter Lane in London, which first met on May 1, 1738. Religious societies were very much a part of the German Pietist tradition, and they had become somewhat popular in London after the Glorious Revolution of 1688. They were both a mark of the religious vitality of England, showing how serious some people were about their spiritual lives, and a critique of the established church, showing how inadequate its ministry was to such people. This society would become a source of both strength and controversy for Wesley over the next couple of years.

A few days later, Peter Böhler left for America and Wesley continued to preach about and wrestle with the idea of true faith. On May 24, 1738, Wesley found (in some measure at least) the goal that he was seeking. In what is likely the most famous passage out of Wesley's *Journal*, he describes what happened next in these words:

> In the evening I went very unwillingly to a society in Aldersgate Street, where one was reading Luther's Preface to the Epistle to the Romans. About a quarter before nine, while he was describing the change which God works in the heart through faith in Christ, I felt my heart strangely warmed. I felt I did trust in Christ, Christ alone for salvation, and an assurance was given me that he had taken away *my* sins, even *mine*, and saved *me* from the law of sin and death.[10]

Here Wesley received the emotional or intuitive assurance of faith that he had lacked earlier but which Peter Böhler had assured him was part of Christian faith. As he narrates the tale further in his *Journal*, he does not describe his new state as one free of temptation or as one in which he felt himself to be more holy. Instead, he notes that he was more open to the power of God in his life.

> After my return home I was much buffeted with temptations; but cried out, and they fled away. They returned again and again. I as often lifted up my eyes, and he "sent me help from his holy place." And herein I found the difference between this and my former state chiefly consisted. I was striving, yea fighting with all my might under the law, as well as under grace. But then I was sometimes, if not often, conquered; now, I was always conqueror.[11]

The Start of the Evangelical Revival

Within a few weeks, Wesley decided to take a trip to Germany, to the home of the Moravians in a town called Herrnhut, near the border of what was then Bohemia (present-day Czech Republic). He wanted to learn more about this newfound—or newly reanchored—faith and to find further testimony of its reality in others. The journey occupied the entire summer of 1738, with Wesley leaving London June 13 and not returning until September 16. In his travels,

Wesley saw Lutheran Pietism firsthand, especially set against the background of the orthodox Lutheranism and Roman Catholicism that surrounded it. His *Journal* during these months is filled with notes of his travels, testimonies from those he met, and commendations about the work of God in the places he saw. These are set next to critiques of the more formal Protestantism and Roman Catholicism that were the main strands of Christianity in Germany.

That summer, Wesley digested the Moravian teachings on faith, and he says that he learned a lot about inward and heartfelt religion from Moravian sermons and testimonies. On returning home, however, he soon began to see clear differences between his Anglican-nurtured faith and that of Lutheran Pietism. On the one hand, many people responded to this "new" idea of salvation by faith, which God may give in an instant. On the other hand, the idea challenged the long-standing Anglican emphasis on behavior in the Christian life. It also struck many Anglicans as a kind of enthusiasm, a set of strong feelings about religion but ones that did not correspond to any of its realities.

To better compare Moravian ideas with those of his own tradition, John Wesley began, in mid-October 1738, to search the official sermons and articles of faith of the Church of England in order, in his words, "narrowly to inquire what the doctrine of the Church of England is concerning the much controverted point of justification by FAITH."[12] He then published extracts from these sources as a pamphlet called *The Doctrine of Salvation, Faith, and Good Works.*[13] He also wrote an extensive and critical letter to the leader of the Moravians, Count Zinzendorf, analyzing Moravian behavior from his time with them, though he waited a year and edited the letter thoroughly before he sent it.

While Wesley continued to wrestle theologically with the meaning of faith and his own experience of it, he continued to preach—mostly in Oxford and London—and to meet with the Fetter Lane Society and with others. His *Journal* highlights these struggles, at one point even finding Wesley claiming that he still wasn't a Christian if measured against the high standard that word seemed to imply.[14] Still, he proclaimed the gospel as he saw it in every place he was invited to preach, but those invitations became fewer and fewer as more and more Anglicans struggled with the oddity of Wesley's message.

Then, in March of 1739, George Whitefield decided that preaching about salvation by faith could not be confined to church services and church buildings, and so he began a practice that was to become characteristic of the growing revival: field preaching. Whitefield would preach in the open air to whomever

decided to stop and hear him, and many of those who stopped were people who
did not go to church or pay much attention if they did. Whitefield soon urged
Wesley to visit him in Bristol so that Wesley could help with the growing work
in that town and see for himself this new evangelistic technique.

Wesley's response was tentative. In his words, "I could scarce reconcile myself at first to this *strange way* of preaching in the fields, of which he set me an
example on Sunday, having been all my life (till very lately) so tenacious of every
point relating to decency and order that I should have thought the saving of
souls *almost a sin* if it had not been done *in a church.*"[15] This attitude, however,
evaporated quickly. The very next day after witnessing Whitefield's field preaching Wesley, in his words, "submitted to 'be more vile,' and proclaimed in the
highways the glad tidings of salvation, speaking from a little eminence in the
ground adjoining to the city, to about three thousand people."[16]

While Wesley and Whitefield now agreed on the means of sharing the gospel, they did not see that gospel the same way. Whitefield was a convinced
Calvinist who believed that God had, from the beginning of creation, predeter-
mined the set number of those who would be saved. Wesley, on the other hand,
saw that as unjust. He was more convinced by the Arminian (or Catholic) view,
in which God gave people free choices and offered grace to anyone who would
accept it. This theological controversy, which had been flaring up and dying
down since the fifth century, would become one of the central theological concerns of Wesley's career.

Wesley realized that this disagreement was significant, but he was unsure
about making it public. In a letter back to the Fetter Lane Society in London,
Wesley recounts these doubts and his decision to determine God's will by cast-
ing lots. This he did on April 26, 1739, and the lot that he drew said, "Preach
and Print." Wesley took this outcome for divine permission not only to proclaim
the doctrine of free grace to all in his preaching but also to publish—much to
Whitefield's dismay—his sermon "Free Grace" three days later.

With the start of field preaching and Wesley's explicit avowal of an Arminian message opposed to predestination, the main ingredients for his role in the
nascent Evangelical Revival were in place, with all of its attendant fruits and
controversies. Nurturing this revival, organizing its fruits, and engaging its controversies now became John Wesley's life's work.

five
Development and Controversy
(1739-49)

The decade of the 1740s saw Methodism come together as a distinct movement within the larger movement that was the Evangelical Revival as Wesley articulated his positions on the various controversies that the revival raised. The basic connectional structure of Methodism took shape as converts were gathered together in societies and bands and as the leaders gathered for annual conferences. Theological controversies arose as Wesley articulated his unique positions on faith and salvation over and against those offered by the Moravian or Calvinist wings of the revival or even his own established church. Other more practical controversies arose, too, as Wesley chose innovative and provocative solutions to the problems he faced in nurturing his growing movement. In any event, more and more people throughout England began to hear about and be affected by the work of both John and Charles Wesley, and by the end of the decade, the movement had adopted an identity that would endure—in spite of many ongoing struggles—for as long as Wesley lived.

All of the events that contributed to the doctrinal and institutional identity of Methodism were interwoven, but telling their story in a strictly chronological way can be confusing. With so many things happening at once, it is hard to hold up all of the incomplete strands of the tapestry of Methodism at the same time and still make sense of the picture. So, for the sake of ease of understanding—but with the warning that the reality was much more complicated than we are presenting it—we will treat these threads separately. We will begin with the development of the structure of Methodism, which embodies ideas that still have much to offer those interested in ministry today. We will then treat three important controversies over ideas that Wesley's early preaching and writing raised: his conflicts with the Anglicans over "enthusiasm" and innovation, his conflict with the Moravians over faith and assurance, and his conflict with the Calvinists over salvation. Since we are also concerned with Wesley as a person, and not just as the iconic leader of Methodism, we will conclude the chapter with the significant events of Wesley's personal life. This outline should help us understand this crucial decade for Wesley, but we must always remember that what we artificially separate for our convenience was never separated in Wesley's experience. He had to juggle all of these issues and problems at the same time.

The Development of the Structure of Methodism

One of the most important things to happen during the decade of the 1740s was the appearance of those practices and institutional structures that would give Methodism its distinctive character. As Wesley tried to live out his fundamental convictions and intuitions about the task to which he felt God had called him, he found the traditional ways of "doing ministry" to be inadequate. Something new was needed. While Wesley did not come up with all these innovations himself, it was still his endorsement of them that gave them their place in the growing Methodist movement. Two of the most important—and therefore most controversial—new practices were field preaching and the use of lay ministers. The most important institutions to develop within Methodism were the society-class-band structures for furthering the spiritual growth of the revival's converts and the annual conference of its leaders. which Wesley used to keep the movement united and focused. We will treat each of these four items in turn.

Field Preaching

As we have already seen, Wesley got the idea of field preaching—basically any preaching done outside of the church—from George Whitefield. Wesley's Anglican prejudices made him leery of the practice, but when he saw its fruits, he surrendered those prejudices and embraced it. From April 1739 until the end of his life, Wesley's *Journals* are filled with the narratives of his travels—the places he preached and the large crowds that came to hear him. More than anything else, it was this practice that gave Wesley access to the ears of those who were least religious, least connected to the structures of the established church, and so perhaps most open to Wesley's "new" message of salvation by grace through faith.

Starting in and around Bristol in the west of England, then by 1742 up north to Leeds and Newcastle, Wesley preached wherever he could find gatherings of people, up to thousands at a time according to his *Journal*. In Bristol, when people responded to his message, he directed them to societies like the ones he had helped form in London. Within a month, the response was so strong that Wesley had to find places where they could build permanent structures to house these new society meetings. Soon, the Methodist movement had its own buildings.

Not all responses were positive, and Wesley records in his *Journal* over the next few years incidents of abuse and mob violence. Once, a bull was let loose among the listeners in Pensford, but throwing stones or whatever else was around was more common. Wesley would complain to the magistrates about their inability to keep the peace, and scoffers reviled these open-air meetings in pamphlets and newspapers, but people still responded and the Methodist movement grew in numbers.

Lay Ministry

Wesley knew that the task of caring for all the people who were coming to faith and of preaching to those who had yet to do so was a task that he alone could not handle. Being the ordained minister that he was, he first hoped that there would be other ministers who would catch the vision of this evangelistic ministry and lend their aid and that this would be enough. This hope, however, proved to be futile. And so, in order to meet the practical need presented by so many people who needed spiritual care and direction, Wesley began to turn to dedicated laypeople to fill the gap that ordained ministers would not fill.

As it was with field preaching, Wesley was first against the idea of having unordained people actually preaching and teaching. When one of his lay helpers in 1740 began to take it upon himself to preach in London in Wesley's absence, he apparently complained to his mother, saying, "Thomas Maxfield has turned preacher, I find." Susanna, who shared many of her son's high church views, responded, "John, you know what my sentiments have been; you cannot suspect me of favouring readily anything of this kind; but take care what you do with respect to that young man, for he is as surely called of God to preach as you are. Examine what have been the fruits of his preaching, and hear him also yourself."[1] Once again, practice overcame prejudice, and Wesley later rejoiced to see God working outside of the boundaries of the official church. Other early lay leaders included John Cennick in Bristol and Joseph Humphreys in London.

Small Groups

In the early 1740s, the groups these laypeople led were also evolving as structures. The original Methodist societies were very similar to the unofficial religious societies that had sprung up in England over the previous fifty years, inspired at least in part by the Lutheran Pietist tradition and the work of Philipp Jakob Spener.[2] These groups met to hear lectures on faith or scriptural expositions and to pray. They were, like the societies that the Moravians were founding, an ordinary supplement to the religious life offered by churches. Wesley wanted his societies to be open to anyone who wanted "to flee from the wrath to come," and he described them as "a company of men 'having the form and seeking the power of godliness.'"[3]

Eventually, these societies began to be divided up into smaller groups as various other communal and spiritual needs arose. In February 1742, while discussing how to pay off the debt on the society meeting place in Bristol (called the New Room), one Captain Foy suggested that everyone give a penny a week. To facilitate this fund-raising exercise, the whole society was divided into groups of twelve, called classes, and each group was appointed a leader to collect the money for the group. In the course of visiting their members to obtain these collections, some class leaders discovered evidence of sins or improper behaviors, and so the class leaders were given responsibility for pastoral oversight of their members as well. This served both to strengthen the accountability with the community and to provide positions of substantial lay leadership within the group.

Because the spiritual needs of the various members of the group also differed, other subdivisions within the society were also soon to arise. Smaller groups of like-minded or like-situated people (single men, for example, or married women) were also encouraged to meet for mutual support, much as Wesley himself had done in the Holy Club at Oxford and as he had encouraged previously in his ministry, even in Georgia. These groups were usually called bands. In some places, a "select society" also arose, composed of the most spiritually advanced members who met to encourage one another to even greater depths of love for God and service to their neighbors.

The Annual Conference

Before too long, Wesley's movement had grown to the point where he decided to include other people in its leadership, consulting them on various issues and working with them on its various problems. And so, in 1744, Wesley invited the other ministers who were helping him in the movement to a conference, which quickly turned into an expected and yearly exercise. The first annual conferences were composed simply of those people that Wesley invited and whose input he sought, and he did not at first see himself creating a new level of organization for the movement. Looking back, however, he eventually said that this is exactly what happened.

The Anglicanism of Wesley's day was very decentralized and static. Its central governing body had not met for a while, and there was little sense that churches or dioceses needed to work together to accomplish God's mission. Each parish functioned, under its bishop, largely on its own. Wesley's movement, however, was dynamic and driven by a strong sense of mission, and so it was almost natural for it to develop structures that would keep everyone headed in the same direction. Though the annual conference began with only the other ordained ministers involved, it eventually grew to include lay leaders too. Each year, Methodist leaders would gather to evaluate their work, assign preachers to the different society circuits, and think together over the theological and practical issues that were important to them. Early concerns included discussions about Calvinism and the need for continued training of their largely untrained group of preachers.

Though Wesley had an undoubtedly strong personality, the group appears to have functioned rather collegially. It was Wesley's initiative, after all, that brought the group together, and there was little sense in calling people together unless he really wanted to hear what they had to say. Eventually, though it would take decades, the annual conference evolved into the group that would direct Methodism—first as a movement, then as a separate denomination—after Wesley's death.

Perhaps more than anything else, it was Wesley's community organization that allowed his movement to both deepen and endure. There were other evangelical preachers like Wesley who proclaimed the gospel, but they did not always nurture their converts or organize their work. Near the end of his life, George Whitefield is said to have recognized this deficiency in his own ministry. Despite his great evangelistic success, he said, "My Brother Wesley acted wisely. The souls that were awakened under his ministry he joined in class, and thus preserved the fruits of his labor. This I neglected, and my people are a rope of sand."[4]

In addition to developing communities, there were other ways in which Methodism grew and left its mark on English society. Many of Wesley's societies, like Wesley himself, had a keen interest in helping the poor and underprivileged. In 1746, the society in London started a medical dispensary to aid the poor, and about the same time Wesley published—as inexpensively as he could—his collection of home remedies called *Primitive Physick* to help those who could not afford a professional physician. In 1748, Wesley and the society in Bristol worked to found a school for the children of coal miners at Kingswood. Eventually, this school would be opened to include the children of Wesley's preachers, and it remains a Methodist boarding school even today.

All of these developments make sense in the light of Wesley's basic theological convictions about the communal nature of Christianity and the importance of active love for God and neighbor, ideas we will explore in more detail in the second half of this book. There were, however, more immediate theological issues at stake that shaped the early growth of the movement, and so it is to these that we must now turn.

Theological Controversies

The growth of Methodist societies and the spread of Methodist ideas did not sit well with all of the religious population of England at the time. There were three particular controversies that marked the early years of Wesley's participation in the Evangelical Revival, and though they were all swirling around Wesley simultaneously, we will treat them separately for clarity's sake. First, there were the disputes about the nature of "church" that arose within Wesley's Church of England due to his unorthodox methods mentioned above. Second, there was a controversy with the Moravians over the nature of faith, doubt, and the practice of "stillness." Finally, there was a controversy with the Calvinist wing of the Evangelical Revival, mainly led by George Whitefield, over the doctrines of predestination and Christian perfection.

Anglican Conflicts over Church

From the very beginning of his movement, Wesley had to fend off criticism from the established church regarding both his message and the means by which he promoted it. Wesley often insisted that there was nothing doctrinally new about his message,[5] but not many of his Anglican colleagues saw it that way. The list of people who wrote against Wesley during this time is long and distinguished, ranging from important bishops to an anonymous but thoughtful correspondent with the pseudonym Mr. John Smith. Even his older brother, Samuel, censured him. Most of their concerns revolved around the implication of Wesley's practices for the idea of church. If one could preach in the open air, what was the use of church buildings? If laypeople could preach, what was the use of ordination? If one could say, as Wesley did, "I look upon *all the world* as *my parish*,"[6] why did the Church of England's systems of order matter? And if religion really were a matter of personal feelings and the heart of an individual, why would the church even matter at all?

Some of these critiques stemmed from misunderstandings, and Wesley wrote as much as he could to clear them up, though not always with success. Still, his *Earnest Appeal to Men of Reason and Religion* (1743) and his *Farther Appeal* (1744-45) are some of the clearest explanations he wrote of Methodism and Christianity, and he would refer back to them for the rest of his life. Other critiques, however, were just, at least from the standpoint of traditional Anglican religion, and Wesley's response was simply to point out how his approach was better. Saving souls, not keeping order, was supposed to be the business of the church. Once, Wesley was denied the use of his father's church in Epworth and ended up preaching from his gravestone instead. "I am well assured," Wesley writes of the event, "I did far more good to them by preaching three days on my father's tomb than I did by preaching three years in his pulpit."[7]

The matter of religious feelings was more complicated, especially because some of Wesley's early evangelistic meetings were punctuated by remarkable displays of people shouting or groaning or even having fits. Eventually, such incidents died down and Wesley developed a nuanced way of balancing his concern with "inward religion" with the external structures designed to promote and preserve it. He always insisted, however, that these feelings and intuitions were part of a personal relationship with God. In fact, they were the very things often missing from the kind of academic faith that his tradition usually offered.

Wesley never developed an easy relationship with the structures of his home church. On the other hand, the church never officially censured him or kicked him out, and he never officially left it. While these early controversies showed some of the weaknesses of the Anglican system, they also forced Wesley to think carefully about his own. In the end, both sides seemed to have benefitted from their interactions with the other. It is unclear that the same is true for the second set of controversies we will look at, the ones Wesley engaged in with the Moravians.

Moravian Conflicts over Faith

As we have already seen, Wesley found his evangelical faith by interacting with the Moravians, and he cared enough about their example to visit them in Herrnhut. However, we have also seen that, upon his return, he began to realize that their perspective on faith created problems for him and others, especially in the society at Fetter Lane. Over the next two years, tensions between Wesley and the Moravians grew until, in July 1740, he was excluded from the Fetter Lane Society altogether. Along with other former members of the Fetter Lane Society, most of them women, Wesley relocated his ministry to another society he had founded the year before, this one at an old ammunition foundry. The Foundry would then become the center of Wesley's London ministry for the next forty years.

Once he was excluded from Fetter Lane, Wesley's relationship with the Moravians deteriorated even further, especially when he finally sent that critical letter he had drafted when he returned from Herrnhut. Wesley continued to be impressed and humbled by the Christian walk of Moravians like Peter Böhler and August Spangenberg, but he could not agree with the approach to faith by the group as a whole. In September 1741, Wesley met with Count Zinzendorf in London to discuss their differences, and he recorded the conversation, which was conducted in Latin, in his diary.[8] After that, Wesley's Methodists and Zinzendorf's Moravians had little to do with each other, though they both continued to conduct society-based ministry in London. By 1745, things had grown so cold that Count Zinzendorf denied any connection between them.

Two things separated Wesley from the Moravians. First, Wesley maintained that there could be degrees of faith and trust in God, with each deeper degree of faith granting a deeper freedom from fear and doubt. This the Moravians denied. To them, faith was an all-or-nothing proposition. If one had any doubt at all, then one had no faith at all. Where Wesley emphasized the progressive side of one's growth in grace, the Moravians insisted that everything happened in an instant and that the new believer at that moment received all that he or she would ever receive from God. Wesley found this opinion destructive of a pursuit of holiness, as well as incompatible with his own experience, and so he rejected it.

Second, they disagreed over how one received this faith from God. Given their orientation toward God's instantaneous work, the Moravians felt that the best way to make room for God's gift of faith was to give up all means of trying to obtain it for oneself. Instead of reading the Bible, taking Communion, and trying to live a Christian life in the world, the Moravians insisted that one could only "be still" and wait passively for God. Since they felt one could not perform religious actions without relying on them, they encouraged people not to read the Bible, not to pray, and not to take Communion until God had given them faith.

Given Wesley's own halting struggle toward faith, he might have easily agreed with the Moravians and considered all his own struggles useless until God had given him faith. Wesley, however, felt just the opposite. He saw all of his feeble efforts toward faith—his trying to practice Christian virtues, his reading of the Bible, and his attending to the means of grace—as the very instruments God used to bring about that deepening work in his own life. When he observed the lives of those who did follow Moravian doctrine—who sat in "stillness" waiting for God to give them faith—he found they often grew cold and moved away from, instead of toward, God. Once again, it was in Wesley's attempts to live out his faith that he determined what ideas did and did not work.

Calvinist Conflicts over Grace

The third major controversy that occupied Wesley's attention during the early part of the 1740s was his debate with the Calvinists. As we saw in the previous chapter, this began when Wesley published "Free Grace" in 1739. This sermon challenged the Calvinist notion of predestination by emphasizing the Arminian (or Catholic) notion that God offered grace to everyone. This was no minor disagreement, as both parties felt the very foundation of the gospel to be at stake. For Wesley, free grace was designed to empower a free and loving response from human beings, leading them to pursue holiness, which was what Christ had come to establish. For the Calvinists, any emphasis on freedom was a denial of the power of grace in salvation, robbing God of the glory due God alone as the sole Author of salvation, whose grace was all-sufficient. In fact, Wesley's ideas sounded like works-righteousness and a denial of the fundamental Protestant belief in justification by faith. Though neither Wesley nor Whitefield wanted a public controversy, there was little hope of keeping so great a disagreement private.

Whitefield waited almost two years to respond to "Free Grace." Finally, someone published a letter he had written to Wesley—but never sent—and distributed it to the members of the Foundry society in early 1741. Claiming that the letter should be treated as a private one, Wesley encouraged his followers to tear it up. This public dismissal of Whitefield's concerns so angered Whitefield that he himself published a sustained critique of Wesley in March of 1741, titled *A Letter to the Rev. Mr. John Wesley in Answer to His Sermon Entitled "Free Grace."* Wesley responded by abridging a couple of already-published works against predestination and distributing them to both his and Whitefield's followers.[9] Whitefield's letter also led Susanna Wesley to write her only published work, an anonymous defense of her son's theology and ministry.

Once this initial flurry of theological activity died down, Wesley and Whitefield tried to keep their relationship civil and cooperate as much as they could in the work of the Evangelical Revival. By the end of the 1740s, they were back on tolerably good terms, though the controversy between them was by no means over. The two were also bound together in their friendship to Lady Selina Hastings, Countess of Huntingdon, with whom Wesley began to correspond in 1741. Lady Huntingdon was a remarkable woman in her own right, and she would become the most important supporter of the Calvinist wing of the Evangelical Revival over the next several decades, which would also lead to further conflicts with Wesley.

Personal Developments

In the midst of these controversies, Wesley was also developing as a person, responding to the conflicts and events around him. Sometimes he recorded his responses in his diary; other times we can only speculate how these things made him feel. In any event, sharing his personal trials is important if we want to see Wesley as a person and not just as the iconic founder of Methodism and champion of Arminian theology. While he enjoyed success in his theological and practical ministry, his personal life during this decade was more often marked by disappointment and loss.

Family Loss

The decade began in a difficult way for Wesley's family, as he lost his oldest brother, his youngest sister, and his mother in less than three years. Samuel

Wesley Jr., who had been the most well established of the Wesley children—the one, apparently, who loaned the rest of his family money—passed away unexpectedly on November 6, 1739. Wesley noted in his *Journal* that his sister-in-law was deep in mourning but that he and his brother Charles rejoiced because their brother had eventually found that assurance of faith in Christ that they preached about but which he at first resisted.

Sixteen months later, on March 9, 1741, Wesley's youngest sister, Kezia (Kezzy), also passed away in her early thirties. Wesley learned of the event from Charles, who reported her end to be peaceful even though her life had been cut short. John does not comment in his *Journal* at the time, but in later letters to his brother-in-law Westley Hall, he blames him for her death. Hall had originally been engaged to Kezzy before breaking off the engagement to marry another of Wesley's sisters, Martha (Patty), in 1735. Wesley believed that the emotional blow Kezzy received from being jilted caused the decline in her health that led to her death.[10]

Then, in July 1742, Susanna Wesley passed away in her apartment at the Foundry. Susanna never had the best of health, and she had been ailing more and more in the years leading up to her death. Since 1740, she had been living with John at the Foundry, where she enjoyed the company, off and on, of all of her living children—though, as she notes in a letter to Charles, not as often as she would have wished.[11] All of them but Charles, who was away on business, were there at the end, and she asked them to sing a hymn of praise to God when she was finally at peace. Wesley records her passing in his *Journal* on July 30, 1742, along with a poetic epitaph written by Charles, celebrating her own experience of finding the assurance of faith.[12]

Though these losses might have affected Wesley personally or emotionally, he did not let them interfere with his evangelistic labors. As we saw above, he labored over the next several years to preach everywhere he could and to organize and maintain the societies that arose from that preaching. He seemed content to do this as a single man until the end of the decade. Then, just over ten years after his failed courtship with Sophy Hopkey, Wesley again found himself romantically entangled. Sadly, this episode, too, was to end in deep disappointment and hurt. If Wesley's personal account is to be believed—and it is the only account that we have—what happened was this.[13]

Romantic Tragedy

In August 1748, Wesley was preaching in Newcastle when he fell ill. There he was nursed back to health by Grace Murray, which was exactly how his relationship with Sophy had begun. Grace was a young widow who worked in the Methodist-run Orphan House and whose job it was to look after "sick and worn out preachers." Wesley developed quite the attraction to her and shared these feelings saying, "If ever I marry, I think you will be the person."[14] Grace was flattered and honored and seemed to return the affection. She accompanied him on his next little preaching tour, after which he left her in the care of one of his assistants, John Bennet. Soon thereafter, Wesley received two letters. One was from Bennet, asking for Wesley's permission to marry Grace. The other was from Grace saying that she felt a marriage to Bennet to be the "will of God."[15]

Wesley was deeply confused, probably not a little hurt, and—given the speed of marriages in those days and the slowness of the post—he figured the two were already married. He gave what he called a "mild answer" and tried to put the whole thing out of his mind. The marriage, however, never took place. In the summer of 1749, Grace was once again with Wesley, this time working with him during his preaching tour of Ireland. During this time, their mutual affections must have rekindled and deepened, because Wesley records that they entered into a quasi-legal verbal marriage contract. When they returned to England, however, Grace heard rumors of Wesley's involvement with another woman and wrote a loving letter to John Bennet in a fit of jealousy. This rekindled Bennet's passion for Grace, and she now found herself torn between two men.

Wesley confronted Grace on the matter in September 1749, and she assured him that she would choose him over Bennet. Wesley wrote to Bennet about the matter, but the letter was never delivered. Charles's copy of the letter, however, was delivered, with dire consequences as we shall see. In the meantime, Wesley continued to wrestle with the propriety of his own actions and affections but came to the determination that it was okay for him to marry and that Grace was the woman. These thoughts, too, he wrote down and sent in a letter to his brother.

When Charles Wesley, who had married earlier that year, received these letters, he was scandalized. Despite his brother's arguments to the contrary, Charles felt that everything would fall apart if Wesley married Grace. She was a servant—thus below his brother's station—and Charles believed that she was already actually married to Bennet, or at least legally betrothed in a way that no longer made her a free woman. To save the Methodist movement from disgrace and his brother from folly, Charles traveled to Newgate. On the basis of other rumors that confirmed his suspicions, Charles personally brought Grace to Bennet and made sure that the two were properly and duly married on October 3, 1749.

When Wesley learned of this, he was stunned. A few days later, upon seeing his brother again, Charles renounced any interaction with him, but Wesley said he felt no anger. His brother's rejection was "only adding a drop of water to a drowning man."[16] Grace later claimed that she thought Charles was taking her to marry Wesley himself. She only agreed to the marriage to Bennet when she was told that Wesley would have nothing more to do with her. The damage, however, was done, and Wesley would have little to do with Grace after that. Just a few days later, in a letter to a friend, he wrote, "Since I was six years old, I never met with such a severe trial as for some days past."[17] With a keen sense of his own misfortune, he wrote in his private journal, "Hardly has such a case been since the beginning of the world."[18] His subsequent letters to Bennet are clearly emotional, and even when they offer forgiveness, they still show just how deeply Wesley had been hurt.[19]

And so a decade that began with public controversy and saw so much positive development in the Methodist movement ended with private tragedy and a rift between Wesley and his brother that was not soon healed. Wesley's decision to marry, however, was not changed. He fulfilled it just a year and a half later, though the result was enough to make us wonder if such a decision was wise. That, however, is a story we will take up as the next decade begins.

six

Settling In and Moving Forward
(1750-69)

---

*F*rom this point, we will pick up our narrative pace as we walk through Wesley's life. It is not that less happened during the last half of Wesley's life as compared to the first. Wesley continued to travel and preach until the year before his death. He continued to write and edit as he created resources for his movement, expounded his ideas, and responded to controversy. But from about 1750, the general course of his life is set and his activity remains very consistent with the pattern established in the 1740s.

Wesley's *Journal* for these twenty years reads like a travelogue as he visits various English towns and even goes to Ireland. Wherever he travels, he preaches outdoors and engages with the various Methodist societies he encounters. When not doing these things, he's reading—something he often did on horseback—or writing and editing. To take one representative example, we find Wesley, as he waits for a tide to turn on a trip to Ireland, translating a logic textbook from Latin for use with his preachers and at the Kingswood school. Earlier he had been working on a French grammar, and after the trip he edited a short introduction to Roman history.[1] By 1750, Wesley had already published a large collection of extracts of devotional works that he called *The Christian Library*, which made many spiritual resources more easily accessible to his people, and he continued this kind of work through the 1750s and 1760s as well. Positive evaluations of Wesley's life often praise his seemingly limitless energy and drive. Less favorable ones paint him as a demanding workaholic. Either way, however, there is no denying that these were very active and productive years for Wesley's ministry.

In the midst of this ongoing pattern of preaching, society work, reading, and writing, there were a number of new and noteworthy developments, and it is on these that we will focus as we continue our journey through Wesley's life. We will begin where we left off in the last chapter, tracing Wesley's personal life through the decades of the 1750s and 1760s. We will then turn to Wesley's ongoing theological controversies, mostly with the Calvinists and the issues that kept bringing them together and then pushing them apart. Finally, we will see how Methodism continued to develop as a movement and institution, one with an increasingly contentious relationship to its parent church.

Personal Life

During this time, Wesley was closely connected to the family of one Vincent Perronet, vicar of Shoreham, about twenty miles southeast of London. His sons, Charles and Edward, became Methodist preachers, and Edward is probably best known as the author of the hymn "All Hail the Power of Jesus' Name." Through them, Wesley came to know a middle-aged widow named Mary Vazeille. Mrs. Vazeille had been married to a prosperous London merchant, who, when he died, had left her enough money to be moderately well-off by the standards of the day. Charles Wesley described her, upon meeting her, as a "woman of sorrowful spirit,"[2] but something about her drew Wesley's attention. He corresponded with her in a pastoral way while he was again preaching in Ireland in the late spring and early summer of 1750. However, sometime after he returned, he began to consider her as a potential life partner. It had been only a year since the tragic end of his romantic relationship with Grace Murray, but Wesley apparently still felt convinced in his logic that it would better for him to marry than to remain single.

Wesley mentions little of this relationship in his *Journal*, so we do not know much about their courtship through the late fall and early winter of 1750-51. We know that Wesley consulted with a few friends about the suitability of this match—most notably Perronet, who gave his full approval. However, we also know that Wesley did not follow his own rules for the marriage of Methodist preachers, which demanded that such unions be approved by the societies among whom the preacher worked. Wesley simply informed his brother that he intended to marry, though he did not say to whom, perhaps fearing a repeat of Charles's unhappy intervention.

On February 9, 1751, Wesley and Mary signed a prenuptial agreement, which stated that her inherited fortune would be settled on her children and not Wesley. The next day, Wesley suffered a bad fall on ice while walking over the London Bridge and ended up recuperating for the week at Mary's house. Just over a week later, on either February 18 or 19,[3] they were married. Wesley does not record anything of the event in his *Journal.*

Letters between John and Mary Wesley demonstrate some real affection between them, but they also make it clear that John had no intention of changing his life of itinerant preaching now that he was married. His correspondence contains as many instructions to a business or ministry partner as they do romantic sentiments. In the first extant letter we have, Wesley tells her, "My dear, be not angry that I put you upon so much work. I want you to crowd all your life with the work of faith and the labour of love."[4] Wesley's friend and sympathetic early biographer Henry Moore noted, "He [Wesley] has more than once mentioned to me, that it was agreed between him and Mrs. Wesley, previous to their marriage, that he should not preach one sermon, or travel one mile the less on that account. 'If I thought I should,' said he, 'my dear, as well as I love you, I would never see your face more.'"[5]

Despite this businesslike cast to their relationship, Mary and John Wesley seemed to have gotten along well at first. When he was sick enough in November 1753 to even write his own epitaph, Mary nursed him back to health.[6] During his travels, either she accompanied him or he kept in touch with her by letter. However, his wife was not Wesley's only female correspondent, and this caused troubles for the rest of their marriage.

In 1754, a young lady with a checkered past was converted under Wesley's ministry. Her name was Sarah Ryan. In 1757, Wesley employed her as a housekeeper in Kingswood and began to keep a regular correspondence with her. While there is nothing particularly scandalous in these letters, they indicate that Wesley and Ryan had an affectionate, as well as pastoral, friendship. When Mary Wesley opened one of these letters from Sarah to her husband, she became jealous enough to leave her husband, vowing never to return.

Mary returned a few days later, but the next few years were rocky in the relationship between Wesley and his wife. She accused him of neglect and apparently broke into his locked desk to get at his correspondence. Wesley then accused her of showing compromising material to his critics. This domestic squabbling eventually abated however, and by 1763, Wesley is praising his wife in letters to his brother.[7] This happier relationship seems to have continued through 1768, but it was not to last.

Mary Wesley became seriously ill in August of 1768, so ill that people thought she might die. On hearing of this, Wesley returned to London to see her. However, once he saw that her life was not in danger—which apparently only took an hour's visit—he headed out again to the upcoming annual conference in Bristol. Wesley, it seems, did have real concern for his wife, but his work held a greater claim on his time and actions. Within a few months, Mary decided she could not live with those priorities and left to go live with her daughter in Newcastle.

Wesley was not the only member of his family having marital difficulties during these decades. Around 1755, the husband of Wesley's sister Martha, the Rev. Westley Hall, left his wife to go to Barbados with a mistress. This left Wesley and his brother Charles to care for Hall's son, their nephew. Sadly, the boy only lived a short while longer, dying at the young age of fourteen. At the same time, Wesley was also providing for another "relation" named Suky Hare, who seems to have been Rev. Hall's illegitimate child. From his letters, we see that his sister's marital troubles troubled Wesley as well.

On a brighter note, these decades saw Wesley befriend a young Swiss immigrant named John Fletcher. In that young man, the Methodist movement found both an excellent example of its ideals as a revivalist movement within the Church of England and its first creative theologian beyond the Wesley brothers themselves. Fletcher was born in 1729 in Switzerland, studied at the staunchly Calvinistic University of Geneva, and moved to London in 1752 to become a tutor for a well-to-do family. After hearing a woman street preacher, he sought out the Methodists and quickly became acquainted with John and Charles Wesley. He listened to Wesley's preaching at the Foundry and had his own "evangelical conversion." Feeling a call to parish ministry, he was ordained in the Church of England in 1757 and turned down a prosperous appointment at an upscale church to minister instead in a poor area called Madeley, where he would serve for the rest of his life. Fletcher would become Wesley's chief theological defender in the controversies of the 1770s and his personal choice as successor to lead the Methodists.

Theological Controversy

As Wesley's private life was having its ups and downs in the 1750s and 1760s, he was also involved in a number of public controversies, mostly with the Calvinists over predestination and holiness. Wesley and Whitefield tried to maintain a friendship in spite of the issues that kept flaring up between them, and their desire for cooperation managed to contain the controversy, though only until Whitefield's death. In August of 1749, Wesley met with Whitefield and other Calvinist Methodists. Together the two parties produced a private statement of understanding in which they promised to not demean one another, to focus on their common ground, and to keep away from unnecessary controversy. Wesley's *Journal* over the next few months shows a deliberate attempt to keep this common front. For example, Wesley traveled to Leeds in October of 1749 to preach with Whitefield, and they worked together in Lady Huntingdon's chapel in early 1750.

Tensions seemed to arise in the early 1750s, however. Wesley published his lengthy tract *Predestination Calmly Considered* in 1752, which suggests that the issue had again become a point of contention. He also sent Whitefield a strongly worded letter in May of 1753, implying that Whitefield was causing some dissention among Wesley's Methodists. After that, however, Wesley's controversial engagement with the issues surrounding Calvinism was focused on other people. The most notable of these was James Hervey and his defenders, with whom Wesley carried on a cumbersomely titled pamphlet war in the late 1750s and early 1760s.

Not all of Wesley's work during this time was controversial, though the issues raised by his debates with the Calvinists still dominated his literary output. Sometimes, he worked on issues that they could agree on, as with the publication of his longest-focused theological work, *The Doctrine of Original Sin, According to Scripture, Reason and Experience* (1757). More often, however, Wesley's maturing theology led him further away from Calvinist positions, particularly those ideas that he felt could directly impair Christian living. This can be seen in his scathing attack on the idea that grace frees us from having to obey the law, titled *A Blow at the Root; or Christ Stabbed in the House of His Friends* (1762). It can also be seen in his steadfast promotion of the idea that God's grace produces holiness, not just forgiveness, as found in the important sermon "The Lord Our Righteousness" in 1765 and, most especially, in the immensely influential book *A Plain Account of Christian Perfection* in 1766.

Still, although his ongoing debates with Calvinist ideas showed that Wesley was concerned about doing good theology, his personal relationship with Whitefield suggests that he was even more concerned about the ongoing work of evangelism. From 1755 on, Wesley speaks of his relationship to Whitefield, particularly in his published *Journal*, in only positive terms, and he took great pains to show that he and Whitefield were partners in the same enterprise. Wesley would occasionally, and a bit triumphantly, remark how much older Whitefield seemed—even though Wesley was ten years his senior—but even still, Wesley's high regard for his revivalist partner and theological rival was clear. Their mutual good relationship was public enough for Wesley to be invited to preach Whitefield's funeral sermon when the latter passed away in 1770, and Wesley publically resolved to only speak good of the man after his death.

The spirit of ecumenism that prevailed between these two men, however, was never to reach an institutional level. During these decades, the Calvinist Methodists had their chapels and preachers and Wesley's Methodists had theirs. In the middle 1760s, Wesley made some deliberate attempts to increase their cooperation by sending out personal letters and eventually a public announcement. When only three preachers responded, however, Wesley basically gave up the effort.

In 1768, however, Countess Huntingdon decided to start a private preacher's college in southern Wales at a place called Trevecca, where she would personally fund the education of pious young men for ministry. Wesley supported the idea. His good friend John Fletcher was appointed the superintendent of the school, and one of his teachers at the Kingswood school was soon made headmaster. It looked like the beginning of a renewed period of cooperation between Wesleyan and Calvinist Methodists, but it was not to last. At the beginning of the next decade, with Whitefield's death and the publication of the minutes of the Annual Conference of 1770, it would all fall apart.

Developments in Methodism

In the midst of personal turmoil and ongoing controversy, Wesley continued to guide his wing of the ongoing Evangelical Revival. His intention had always been to foster an inward and experiential religion that would drive outward holiness within the Church of England. As soon as Wesley's movement became organized, however, the contrasts between Methodism and the Church of England were great enough to engender discussions about leaving that fold and starting a new church altogether. Wesley resisted that decisive move, but his views on church and ministry kept evolving in ways that justified many smaller moves farther and farther away from Methodism's "mother church."

As we saw from his days in Oxford and his ministry in Georgia, Wesley began with a strong set of high church principles, principles that put a lot of weight on proper form and proper conduct as measured by the rules of the church. Little by little, however, Wesley began to prioritize the work of ministry and the goals of the gospel over the formal structures of church. The tension that developed in the 1750s and 1760s between Wesley's idealized view of the Church of England and his consistent, practical violation of its institutional standards would be characteristic of Wesley until the end of his life.

On the one hand, at the end of the 1740s, Wesley published *A Word to a Methodist* and *A Plain Account of the People Called Methodists*, both of which tried to describe the distinctiveness of the Methodist identity as restoring true, scriptural Christianity to the Church of England—not as setting up a separate identity alongside of it. On the other hand, Wesley's reading was giving him reasons to believe that the institutional structures in which the Church of England's identity was embedded—and against which Wesley's movement often struggled—were not as well grounded as he had first believed. In 1746, Wesley read *An Enquiry into the Constitution, Discipline, Unity, and Worship of the Primitive Church* by Lord Peter King. This book claimed that the basic distinction between bishop and elder—a distinction upon which much of the political power in the church was based—was not biblical. In 1750, Wesley read *The General Delusion of Christians with Regard to Prophecy* by John Lacy, which convinced him that the followers of Montanus—a charismatic leader in the late second century, eventually labeled a heretic by the institutional church—were actually "real, scriptural Christians."[8] Wesley's suspicions about the adequacy of the institutional church were further confirmed by his reading *A History of the Councils* by Richard Baxter in 1754 and *The Irenikon* of Edward Stillingfleet the following year.

More and more Wesley grew to believe that the mission of the church—to save souls and help people lead holy lives—was more important than its formal structures, and this made the question of separation from the Church of England a pressing one. Especially at issue was whether or not Methodist preachers, even though laymen, could serve the sacraments, something the Anglican Church only allowed ordained ministers to do. Some preachers, notably Thomas Walsh and Charles Perronet, had already done this. So at the Annual Conference of 1755, held at Leeds, the issue of separation was made the central matter of debate. Wesley prepared an extensive paper on the matter,[9] which he read, and he encouraged all attendees to speak. The gathered group of preachers, about forty of them or so, discussed the matter for several days. Wesley put their conclusion regarding separation in this way: "And on the third day we were all fully agreed in that general conclusion, that (whether it was *lawful* or not) it was no ways *expedient*."[10] So, while the group could not agree theologically whether such a separation was ever justified, they did agree practically that this was not the time for it. Practicality, not theology, formed the basis of their response.

Now, this is not to say that Wesley had no theological reasons for pushing the practical boundaries of his church, and he cared about giving good reasons for his deviations. In a letter the following year to Samuel Walker, he defended lay preaching by claiming that they followed an "inward call," one empowered by the Spirit, which gave them more freedom than a mere "outward call," represented by ordination.[11] That same year, however, he issued a plea to his fellow Church of England ministers called "An Address to the Clergy."[12] In that open letter, he urged all the clergy to live up to the high level of their calling, a calling that Wesley articulated in very Methodist-sounding terms. After the Leeds conference, perhaps Wesley felt that if the clergy of the Church of England were doing their job better, the pressures to separate from it would lessen.

But lessen they did not. Many Anglican bishops found it dangerous to think that people could be led by the Spirit to work outside of the boundary lines of the institutional church. In 1762, Bishop William Warburton of Gloucester issued a critique of Methodism called *The Doctrine of Grace; or The Office and Operations of the Holy Spirit Vindicated from the Insults of Infidelity and the Abuses of Fanaticism*. Apparently wanting a true debate on the matter, Bishop Warburton let Wesley read a draft of the work before it was published. After its publication, Wesley issued a lengthy response[13] in which he tried to balance the concerns of both structure and spirit, though he still gave a clear priority to the latter.

That balance, however, was very hard to maintain. On the one hand, Wesley distanced himself from the institutional forces of the Church of England and justified those moves by appealing to the leadership of the Holy Spirit. Ironically, however, at the same time he was forced into greater institutionalization within his own movement by those who—at least in Wesley's eyes—took the logic of Spirit leading too far. The two most conspicuous examples of this were the lay preachers George Bell and Thomas Maxfield.

George Bell was converted by Methodist ministry in 1758 and very soon thereafter felt a call to preach. What he preached and the way he preached it, however, immediately began to cause trouble for Wesley and for the society that met at the Foundry. Bell's message was of a Christian perfection that elevated the believer above all regulation, all law or standard of behavior. This message did not sit well with Wesley, nor did the hyperemotional way that Bell preached it, ranting and raving and shouting from the pulpit. Wesley tried to correct his errant preaching, but to no avail. After Bell proclaimed that the world would end on February 28, 1763, Wesley confronted him, and Bell and his followers left the society.

About the same time, the preaching of Thomas Maxfield was also causing dissention and division in the London Methodist ranks. As we saw in the last chapter, Maxfield was one of the first laypeople whose ministry Wesley recognized as God inspired despite a lack of formal training or church sanction. By the early 1760s, however, he had begun to preach Christian perfection and sanctification in a way that denigrated God's work in justification and nearly equated Christian perfection with a kind of directly inspired Spirit leading. Maxfield, like Bell, had no use for Wesley's authority. In March of 1763 he refused to preach at the Foundry, eventually leaving Methodism altogether to become an independent minister.

These controversies over authority and over the content of the preaching in Methodist societies led the Methodist conference of that year, 1763, to adopt what they called a Model Deed. The Model Deed furthered the institutional development of Methodism by providing a set of standards for the preaching that was to occur in the Methodist societies. That standard was the doctrine put forth in Wesley's four published volumes of sermons and in his *Notes on the New Testament*, a commentary that Wesley had written during the early part of 1754 when his illness prevented him from traveling and preaching.

Still, even while Methodism continued to institutionalize, Wesley could not yet bring himself to fully act out the priority of function over form. In 1765, the need for ordained ministers within the Methodist movement had been rising, and the movement received little help from Anglican sources. That year, Wesley secured the services of a Greek bishop to ordain a few of his preachers. In retrospect, Wesley realized that this was not a good idea, and the small scandal that ensued in some local publications led him never to attempt such a compromise again. But the very fact that he did so reveals his own ambivalence about the lengths to which he could or should go to let Methodism develop as a full-blown church independent of the Church of England.

This relationship became even more complicated as Methodism spread beyond the boundaries of England and thus outside the jurisdiction of England's national church. By the time Wesley made his first visit to Ireland in 1747, there were already Methodist societies meeting there. By 1752, there were enough Irish Methodists for them to begin having their own conferences. Wesley would end up making many trips to Ireland over the rest of his life, by some accounts spending a total of six years there in one- to three-month snatches.

From Ireland, Methodism made its way, without Wesley's knowledge, to the New World. Irish immigrant Robert Strawbridge had started Methodist meetings in Maryland by 1766. About the same time, just to the north, Irish Methodists Philip Embury and Barbara Heck worked with one Captain Thomas Webb to start a society in New York. The latter work met with enough success that, in 1768, the society wrote to John Wesley in England, pleading for him to send some qualified workers to help them. Wesley read the letter to the Annual Conference of 1768, and from the annual conference the next year, he would commission two preachers: Richard Boardman and Joseph Pilmore. They arrived near Philadelphia at the end of October 1769 and immediately began preaching and helping to grow the societies there. The work in America would grow amazingly well. However, the looming political and military conflict between England and her colonies would both hamper all of Wesley's efforts to keep American Methodism within the bounds he had set for it in England and force the issue of separation from the Church of England. But that is a story for the next chapter.

seven

Leaving a Legacy
(1770-91)

$\mathcal{T}$he last quarter of Wesley's life was not a time of rest and retirement. Rather, it was as full of activity as any of his previous decades had been. His health stayed remarkably strong until his last couple of years, and he considered all the time given him as time to be used for God. His relentless activity is probably what led to the final collapse of his marriage, but Wesley continued to preach and engage in controversy—particularly with the Calvinists—and tried to direct his movement, both in England and in America, toward a future without him. We will take a brief look at each of these areas in turn as we walk with Wesley through the final decades of his life.

Personal Life

We will begin again with Wesley's personal life and with the final dissolution of his unfortunate marriage. As we noted in the last chapter, Mary had left her famous husband at the end of the 1760s, and his passing references to her in his letters indicate a prolonged absence. She eventually returned, but it was only to leave again. On January 23, 1771, Wesley writes in his *Journal*, "For what cause I know not to this day, [Mrs. Wesley] set out for Newcastle, purposing 'never to return.' *Non eam reliqui; non dismisi; non revocabo* [I did not desert her; I did not dismiss her; I will not call her back]."[1] In August of that year, Wesley writes tellingly to his brother, "My wife, I find, is on the high ropes still. I am full of business, as you may suppose."[2] By the summer of 1772, however, the two were together again, perhaps as a result of Wesley's visit to Newcastle, and their letters over the next couple of years make it seem as though they were on companionable terms, though the correspondence is filled with more business than affection.

In July of 1774, however, Wesley writes a long letter rehearsing the grievances of the past and encouraging Mary to be submissive. This was not acceptable to Mary, however, and she leaves him sometime after that, this time never to return. In the midst of the Calvinist controversy discussed below, she apparently showed some compromising papers of Wesley to his detractors, and this seems to have closed off any real possibility of reconciliation at that point. Wesley's letter to her in 1777 demands that she retract the things she has said publically about him, and his apparently final letter to her in 1778 concludes with these words: "If you were to live a thousand years, you could not undo the mischief that you have done. And till you have done all you can towards it, I bid you farewell."[3]

Mary died in 1781, and Wesley only notes in his *Journal* that he heard about her funeral a day or so after it happened,[4] though it appears she left him a "mourning ring" in her will, "in token that I die in love and friendship toward him."[5] After her death, Wesley's heart may have softened toward her, and he mentions her with a touch of fondness.[6] Nevertheless, Wesley's marriage remains one of the more difficult and puzzling episodes in the career of this eminent, but still very human, evangelist.

The Minutes Controversy

As we hinted in the last chapter, Wesley's relationship with the Calvinist wing of the Methodist movement was headed toward its rockiest days as the final decades of the eighteenth century got under way. The expulsion of six Calvinist Methodist students from St. Edmund's Hall, Oxford, in 1767—the event that gave the final impetus to Lady Huntingdon's founding of the preacher's college at Trevecca—also touched off an exchange within the Methodist movement between Huntingdon's Calvinists and Wesley's Arminians. A major publication in this debate was *The Doctrine of Absolute Predestination Stated and Asserted*, Augustus Toplady's English translation of a Reformation-era work by Jerome Zanchius. All this seemed to renew Wesley's worry, voiced as far back as the first annual conference (1744)—that his movement "leaned too much toward Calvinism."[7]

Apparently out of a desire to spark some debate on the subject, Wesley published a parody of Toplady's translation, perhaps the most uncharitable thing Wesley ever wrote. This set off a flurry of venomous replies from the Calvinists, which in turn made Wesley even more worried about the problem. He raised the issue at the annual conference in August 1770, and those minutes outlined the Wesleyan-Methodist position over and against Calvinism, particularly on the issue of justification by faith and the role of humanity's response to God.

Just over a month later, on September 30, 1770, Whitefield died while on a preaching tour of America, and with him died Wesley's strongest personal connection to the Calvinists. It was Whitefield's wish that Wesley preach his memorial service, which he was duly invited to do in November of that year. In his sermon from Numbers 23—"Let me die the death of the righteous, and let my last end be like his!" (v. 10, KJV)—Wesley tried to take a peaceful tone and emphasize those doctrines on which both he and Whitefield had agreed. He did not mention anything of predestination, however. Given how important that was to Whitefield, that omission was conspicuous and angered Whitefield's supporters. Shortly thereafter, the minutes of the recent annual conference were published, and tensions rose to a whole new level.

At issue was the wording that Wesley and his preachers used to distance themselves from Calvinism. In the minutes, they explicitly denied the statement "a man is to do nothing in order to justification," by saying, "Whoever desires to find favour with God should 'cease from evil and learn to do well.'"[8] The conference may have intended this as a refutation of any antinomianism that would sever the connection between salvation and holy living. However, it was read by Calvinists like Lady Huntingdon as refuting justification by faith and replacing it with justification by works. "Popery unmasked," Lady Huntingdon called it.[9]

Immediately, Countess Huntingdon required all those in her circle to explicitly repudiate the statement. When her headmaster at Trevecca, Joseph Benson, refused to do so, he was let go, and John Fletcher also resigned in support of him. In June 1771, Lady Huntingdon's personal chaplain, Walter Shirley, tried to rally evangelical preachers against Wesley, proposing that they gather in a "counter-conference" at the same time as Wesley's annual conference and confront the group to demand a retraction. Only a few preachers showed up to this counter-conference, however, and Wesley received them politely and listened to their concerns. He prepared a conciliatory document that reaffirmed his belief in justification by faith, and he admitted that the minutes in question had used unguarded language.

Whatever renewed hope for peace that document could have promised, however, was quickly dashed when Wesley published John Fletcher's *A Vindication of the Rev. Mr. Wesley's Last Minutes,* which he did, oddly enough, over both Shirley's and Fletcher's objections. This renewed a controversy that would last for the next several years. Fletcher's *Checks to Antinomianism* held up the Arminian side of the debate, while on the Calvinist side, the main proponents were Augustus Toplady and the brothers Rowland and Richard Hill.

Wesley was implicated in these debates, which became rather ugly at times, but he did not often engage them directly. For this round, he left that work to Fletcher. Instead, we find Wesley regretting the way these debates tore at the Methodist societies.[10] To encourage his followers, Wesley also started a periodical in 1778 that he called *The Arminian Magazine,* whose title only served to keep the controversy in view. Throughout his life, it seems that Wesley wanted to fight for truth as he saw it and also to keep the peace for the sake of evangelism and spiritual growth. But he could never have both.

American Methodism

As we have seen, the story of American Methodism is only tangentially connected to Wesley's personal story. Methodism was founded in the New World without his knowledge, and his influence on that group across the water was always minimal and often resisted. Still, the controversy it sparked is a part of his story, and the independence of American Methodism from Wesley coincides well with the independence of the British colonies from the crown.

In 1768, King George III started stationing soldiers in and around Boston to protect the crown's interests against an increasingly unhappy colonial population. This eventually led to a showdown between protesters and British soldiers in March of 1770, known as the Incident on King Street to the British but popularized as the Boston Massacre in the colonies. The British Parliament's Tea Act of 1773 led to the famous Boston Tea Party, which led to further escalation of the hostilities between Britain and her American colonies. These finally reached the point of open conflict in 1775.

During this time, Wesley contemplated himself coming to America but never found the opportunity. Instead his role in American Methodism consisted in sending a few more preachers from his annual conference for the work, though this was done through volunteers and not by assignment. Most notably among those was the young Francis Asbury, who went in 1771 and was appointed one of the "assistants" or superintendents over the American work. It was Asbury who would become American Methodism's chief organizer and proponent, and this would lead to a clash with Wesley himself.

The American Methodist statistics were recorded by the British annual conference, affirming the connection between them, until the war made communication unreliable. Conference minutes show a growth from 316 society members in 1771 to 3,148 in 1775, a tenfold increase in just four years. The Americans held their first annual conference in Philadelphia in 1773, where they affirmed their connection to Wesley (as opposed to the Calvinist Methodists) and promised to teach his doctrine as contained in his sermons and writings. There was, apparently, already some unease at Wesley's known pro-British stance concerning the colonies, but it seems that this was held in check in the interest of unity. Events moved swiftly, however, and that unity was not to endure.

Open hostilities broke out between the colonists and the British crown in April of 1775. Mentions of America disappear from the annual conference minutes, and most of Wesley's preachers returned to England. Francis Asbury, however, stayed, and this made people look to him for leadership, rather than to Wesley back in England. While Wesley was sympathetic to the American calls for justice, he disliked the calls for independence, because political matters had religious overtones. "Loyalty is with me," Wesley wrote, "an essential branch of religion, and which I am sorry any Methodist should forget. There is the closest connection, therefore, between my religious and my political conduct; the self-same authority enjoining me to 'fear God' and to 'honour the King.'"[11]

During the war years, Wesley published thirteen different sermons and open letters supporting the crown over the colonists. Most significant among these was his *Calm Address to the American Colonies* (1775). The address never made it to America, but it caused quite a commotion back in England and added fuel to the personal attacks against Wesley. Most notable among them was Augustus Toplady's *An Old Fox Tarr'd and Feather'd*, in which he accused Wesley (not without some justice, it must be said) of plagiarizing the bulk of that tract from Samuel Johnson's *Taxation No Tyranny*.

Wesley's anti-independence position complicated matters for the American Methodists, since many assumed that all Methodists followed their founder. This encouraged American Methodists to distance themselves from Wesley's person, however much they might still follow his doctrine. Additionally, official Anglican presence was nearly nonexistent in America during the war, and this created distance between the Methodists and their mother church. Wesley recognized this problem and personally petitioned the bishop of London to ordain more Anglican clergy for America in 1780. His pleas went unheard, however. The gap between Wesley and the American Methodists and between the American Methodists and the Church of England set the stage, once the Treaty of Paris was signed in 1783, for Wesley's most radical move yet in the ongoing question of Methodism's relationship to the Church of England.

The turmoil in America had been good for the growth of Methodism there, more than doubling to about 7,000 members from 1775 to 1778 and again to about 15,000 members from 1778 to 1784. In that year, Wesley finally took matters into his own hands and ordained—on his own authority—two of his preachers, Richard Whatcoat and Thomas Vasey, for the work in America. He also appointed Thomas Coke as a superintendent, giving him authority to appoint Francis Asbury as another superintendent once Coke arrived in America. Wesley then sent with them revised and condensed versions of the Book of Common Prayer and the Church of England's Thirty-Nine Articles of Religion to be used as the foundation of a new church. Since the Americans had thrown off the political rule of Britain, and since the Church of England was tied to that political rule, it hardly made sense to Wesley to try to keep the American Methodists Anglican.[12]

These moves represent the last functional influence Wesley had over the American wing of his movement. When Coke arrived in America, Asbury would not accept a personal ordination from him on behalf of Wesley until it had been approved by the American conference. This ensured that his own leadership would be anchored in the will of the American Methodists and not in Wesley. A couple of years later, in 1786, Wesley tried to get Richard Whatcoat also appointed superintendent and to fix the date for the upcoming American conference. His instructions, however, were ignored, and the American conference that year even eliminated Wesley's name from their minutes, claiming that no one in Europe had any right to dictate affairs in America. Wesley wrote a strongly worded letter to Asbury protesting this and other matters, which pained Asbury but did not change his mind. Wesley reports a few years later in a letter, "He [Asbury] told George Shadford, 'Mr. Wesley and I are like Caesar and Pompey: he will bear no equal, and I will bear no superior.' And accordingly he quietly sat by until his friends voted my name out of the American *Minutes*. This completed the matter and showed that he had no connexion with me."[13] Wesley's name was eventually restored to the American conference minutes, and the Americans upheld his doctrines, but he had no further part personally in the American Methodist story.

British Methodism

As all this was happening in America, equally momentous events were transpiring in Britain, events that would also lead to British Methodism's eventual separation from the Church of England after Wesley's death. At the same time that he helped push Methodism in that direction, however, Wesley was still worried about where it would lead. It was important to him that he remain an Anglican, and he feared that if his Methodists left the Church of England, as Lady Huntingdon's Calvinist Methodists did in 1772, they would "gradually sink into a formal, honourable sect."[14] For Wesley, it was the mission of the Methodists "to spread life among all denominations,"[15] which they could not do if they turned into one themselves. It is, therefore, somewhat ironic that Wesley's focus on that mission led him to act in ways that encouraged the very thing he feared.

Methodism continued to grow in Britain during the last decades of Wesley's life, and with that growth came new challenges. In 1770, there were just over 29,000 members of Methodist societies in the British Isles (including Scotland and Ireland). By 1780, that number was almost 44,000, and the conference following Wesley's death in 1791 reported over 72,000 members. There were struggles over the erection of preaching houses, the paying of various obligations, and the support of the Kingswood school, but there were also times of great celebration. In 1778, the City Road Chapel was completed, and that became the new center of Wesley's movement, replacing the Foundry. Located across the street from the famous Bunhill Fields cemetery, it contains Wesley's personal apartments and "home chapel," and it still draws Methodist "pilgrims" and others even to the present day.

Wesley felt a great responsibility for ensuring the future of Methodism after his death, and so these years find him trying to create a sustainable institution that would fulfill its mission but not leave the Church of England. At first, he hoped that another Anglican clergyman might take over the reins of leadership after him. John Fletcher's conduct during the years of controversy with the

Calvinists in the early 1770s convinced Wesley that Fletcher was the man for the job, and he told him as much. Fletcher declined such a role, however, and so Wesley was forced to consider other options.

In 1784, Wesley finally set up the annual conference of the Methodists as a legal entity, with a seemingly arbitrary one hundred of his nearly two hundred preachers assigned as a "Legal Hundred" with responsibility for oversight over the various societies and preaching houses. He did this through a "Deed of Declaration" that was inserted into the conference minutes for that year. Controversy arose immediately. Many preachers who were excluded from the Legal Hundred were hurt, and some left the movement. Additionally, Wesley did not himself submit to this new authority, and he continued to act as the real authority for the conference, inviting whom he would and appointing preachers as he saw fit.

After his ordination of preachers for America in that same year, Wesley started exercising a bishop-like office at home as well. The next year, Wesley ordained three preachers for work in Scotland, a move he could continue to justify since the Church of England was not technically established there. But by 1788, he had also ordained preachers for work in England, though interestingly enough the accounts of those ordinations never showed up in Wesley's published *Journal*, only in his private diaries.

We see the same tension between staying within the Church of England and chafing against its limits in Wesley's attitude toward holding Methodist meetings at the same time as regular Anglican services. In 1786, Wesley still cautioned his Methodists not to hold services that conflicted with those of the local parish church. However, by 1788 he was making moderate allowances for this, though he claimed it did not mean that Methodists were leaving the Church of England. At the same time, Wesley could also write to the bishop of London, begging him not to drive the Methodists out of the Church of England. Whether this was Wesley trying to hold a very fragile middle ground or trying "to have his cake and eat it, too," is a matter of debate. However, the tension shows how important both realities—the mission of the Methodists *and* their place in the Church of England—were to Wesley.

Aside from separation, Wesley's other main concern about his Methodists toward the end of his life was wealth. For Wesley, that seemed to be the one other thing that could drain the heart of a movement that had found its first real successes among the poor and downtrodden. Many years earlier, Wesley had preached his famous sermon "The Use of Money,"[16] and he himself tried to live by the advice he gave there: "Earn all you can; save all you can; give all you can." His intention was to die with no wealth that anyone could inherit, and he was even known to go begging among his rich friends for money to give to the poor. As he once wrote to a friend, Ann Foard, "I *bear* the rich, and love the poor; therefore I spend *almost all* my time with them!"[17]

Wesley, however, did not feel that this attitude was sufficiently shared by his Methodists. Therefore, near the end of his life, he addressed it in sermons such as "On Dress" (1786), "The Danger of Riches" (1788), "On Worldly Folly" (1790), and "The Danger of Increasing Riches" (1790).[18] He encouraged people to visit the sick and to give money to the poor as much for their own sakes as for the benefit of those they were helping. He was even said to have made disparaging comments on the unnecessary ruffles of one of his preacher's shirts during his last conference.[19] On a positive note, when one of his Methodists, John Gardner, wanted to found the Stranger's Friend Society to help those who had no other means of support—even if they weren't Methodists—Wesley circulated a copy of this society's rules to his other societies and contributed triple the subscription that Gardner had first asked for.[20]

Related to Wesley's concern for the poor was his reenergized support for the abolitionist movement against slavery. Wesley had witnessed the horrors of slavery in 1737 while still in America. He never felt good about the practice, but the problem did not occupy much of his attention during the middle part of his life. At the end of his life, however—perhaps fueled by his political opinions about the American Revolution—he addressed the problem again. In 1774, he published a scathing attack on slavery with the deceptively mild title *Thoughts on Slavery*, and he remarked happily in his *Journal* that the American war had at least disrupted the slave trade. In the last few years of his life, he even preached a sermon on slavery (which was, interestingly enough, accompanied by a great storm)[21] and wrote letters of encouragement to those actively involved in abolitionist efforts, including Granville Sharp,[22] who had started an abolition society, and William Wilberforce,[23] who had taken up the cause in Parliament.

There were at least two other significant developments in British Methodism during these final years of Wesley's life in which Methodism took a progressive role compared to its mother church. Interestingly enough, they were not Wesley's original ideas, and—like so many other innovations—he resisted them both at first. However, practice again overcame prejudice, and the promotion of "foreign missions" and the use of women preachers came to be important characteristics of the movement Wesley left behind.

Credit for starting the modern missionary movement usually goes to William Carey, and not without good reason. But at the same time that Carey was thinking about the obligations Christians might have to spread the gospel to foreign lands, one of Wesley's chief ministers, Thomas Coke, was having similar thoughts. Wesley and the rest of his preachers resisted the idea of "wasting" ministerial resources on foreign missions when they were so badly needed at home. The Annual Conference of 1778 declined Coke's idea of sending missionaries to Africa, and a group of preachers that Wesley consulted in 1784 had a similar reaction to missions in the East Indies. Coke kept at it, however, and eventually Wesley began to see that the idea had merit. In 1786, Coke published an exhortation to missions to which Wesley contributed a preface. While no mission work beyond the New World was attempted until after Wesley's death, eventually foreign missions (and its ecumenical derivatives) would become very much a part of Methodist identity.

The other remarkable development during this period was the slow but real acceptance of women as preachers in the Methodist preaching houses. As with the case of lay preaching in the early 1740s, it was circumstances that created the conditions for change. Woman had been leaders in the bands from early on, and in the 1760s, Wesley had given a qualified endorsement to Sarah Crosby's exhortations and testimonies, which function as preaching in all but name. But that name was still important to Wesley, and he encouraged Sarah to affirm this to her hearers and to say the following: "You lay me under a great difficulty. The Methodists do not allow of woman preachers; neither do I take upon me any such character. But I will just nakedly tell you what is in my heart."[24]

By the 1770s, however, Wesley, through the encouragement of Mary Bosanquet (who would later marry John Fletcher), began to allow the justification he had previously used for lay preachers to apply to women preachers as well. Given that God obviously seemed to be using such a ministry, Wesley could affirm that they were given an "extraordinary call," something that went beyond the bounds of the normal and ordinary but still must be accepted. Still, Wesley was sensitive to the exceptional nature of this work and was not interested in allowing it to become "ordinary." In March of 1780, he wrote in a letter to George Robinson, "I desire Mr. Peacock to put a final stop to the preaching of women in his circuit. If it were suffered, it would grow, and we know not where it would end."[25]

But grow it did, apparently. Eventually, the fruits of such labor became fully apparent to Wesley and the rest of his Methodists. Despite the fact that it was still a controversial idea, the Manchester Conference of 1787 officially appointed its first woman preacher to the Norwich circuit, Sarah Mallet, saying, "We give the right hand of fellowship to Sarah Mallet, and have no objection to her being a preacher in our connexion, so long as she preaches the Methodist doctrines, and attends to our discipline."[26]

The End of the Matter

Through most of the tumultuous years described above, Wesley remained remarkably vigorous for a person of his age. His birthday entries in his *Journal* celebrate his ongoing health, and he kept up an active preaching tour, though he found himself using a carriage more and more often instead of riding on horseback. In the middle of 1783 and 1786, he even made two recreational visits to the Netherlands, short pauses from his otherwise nonstop labors.

Age eventually caught up with him, however, though he still outlived his closest friends and all but one member of his family, his sister Martha. John Fletcher died a premature death of fever just shy of his fifty-sixth birthday in 1785. Three years later, Charles Wesley passed away. In working through his late brother's poems at the end of 1788, Wesley remarked in his *Journal* that age was creeping up on him. Now eighty-five years old, he found his eyesight greatly weakened, though he rejoiced that he was not yet a burden, that he could still travel, and that his memory and understanding were not dimmed as far as he could tell.[27] His birthday entry for the next year, 1789, admitted "I now find I grow old," especially noting his failing strength and memory. Wesley's birthday in 1790 was to be his last, and at that point he knew himself to be near the end.

Wesley attended his last annual conference in August 1790. In October, he finished his last preaching tour and published the last section of his *Journal*, though he continued to keep a diary until a week before his death. In November, Elizabeth Ritchie, one of Wesley's younger friends and "adopted daughter," answered his need for a housekeeper and caretaker, and we find her listed almost every day in his diary, reading to him since he could no longer read on his own. It is from her hand that we have an account of Wesley's last days.[28]

Near the end of February 1791, Wesley preached his last sermon. He shortly took ill with a fever, and it was an illness from which he would never recover. By March 1, Wesley's friends knew these were his final days, and they gathered around him. He asked for a pen and paper to write something down, but he did not have the strength to use them. When Elizabeth Ritchie asked him what to write, he replied, "Nothing, but that God is with us." He gathered his strength to sing a hymn, Isaac Watts's "Praise My Maker," one of his favorites, and the words of that hymn lingered on his lips through the night even when he had no more energy to sing them. The next day, March 2, 1791, at ten o'clock in the morning, Wesley breathed his last. He was buried on the grounds of his City Road Chapel, his coffin carried to the grave site, as per his request, by six poor men, who each received a pound for their trouble. "I particularly desire," he noted in his will, "there may be no hearse, no coach, no escutcheon, no pomp, except the tears of them that loved me, and are following me to Abraham's bosom."[29]

So ended the remarkable life of a remarkable man. Beloved by those who felt the positive impact of his Methodist movement, reviled by those who chafed under his leadership or who opposed his theology, John Wesley nevertheless was one of the most successful evangelists and religious organizers that England had ever seen. It was a life that contained its contradictions but also its great insights. And so, with the information of this life in hand, it is time we turned to those thoughts that form his theological legacy.

PART II
JOHN WESLEY'S THOUGHT

Wesley's Theological Method
eight

Having completed our brief overview of Wesley's life, we now turn to his theological legacy. We will begin our tour of Wesley's thought by looking at his orientation toward theology itself. Wesley had a distinct theological method, a pattern of thinking one can use to say something meaningful about God. Theological method discusses the sources a theologian uses and the way he or she generates new conclusions from old starting places. In a way, theological method is like the "grammar" of the language of theology, the rules for putting things together so that they make sense. Knowing *how* theologians did their work helps us understand *what* they wrote about, so theological method gives us a convenient place to start exploring their thought. However, as convenient as it is, we must recognize that it is also artificial.

We did not learn our first language by studying grammar; we learn to speak by speaking. Grammar comes in later to help us understand what we do when we speak. In the same way, Wesley did not figure out a theological method first and then start doing theology. Like most craftsmen, Wesley learned the craft of theology by doing it. Theology for him was never an "ivory tower" discipline in which he figured out all the answers and wrote them down in a book. Instead, Wesley acted as if theology was for the day-to-day business of living the Christian life, messy as that is sometimes. When confronted with an issue, Wesley just jumped in and started doing theology, figuring out what worked and what did not as he went along. Even though he personally had a hard time admitting that he was ever wrong, Wesley's thought still shows distinctive marks of development. That development is marked by a useful set of intuitions and a consistent dynamic pattern that can still help us as we do theology today.

Wesley's theological method is not significant because he figured out something about doing theology that no one before him had. Everything Wesley built theologically, he built with the same tools everyone else was using. Wesley's distinctiveness comes in the way he used those tools and kept in balance several forces that often push theology off track. Two of those balancing acts in particular are important to those who want to follow in Wesley's theological footsteps: the one between academic and practical theology and the one between the sources and tools that feed theological reflection.

To many people, theology sounds like an academic discipline, something far removed from the ordinary life of faith and of the church, but that's not how Wesley treated it. As we have seen, Wesley was trained as an Oxford scholar, but he found a way of doing theology that combined scholarly work with a pastoral orientation. He cared enough about good theology to write pages and pages of it. However, he cared even more about the God to which all that theology was supposed to be pointing, a God who was actively involved in the world to save people. Wesley spent his theological energy on those things that he thought would make the biggest impact. "I design plain truth for plain people," he said.[1] For Wesley, all good theology was practical theology. Academic rigor was always put into the service of pastoral practice. This helps us understand why we find Wesley focusing on some topics—such as sin and salvation—and all but ignoring others.

Wesley's balancing act between academic and practical theology is connected to another one, the one between the various sources and tools for doing theology. This we will explore in much greater depth because it is here that Wesley offers us a model for doing theology that is still productive more than two hundred years after his death. Most theologians recognize that Scripture, tradition, reason, and experience are all important in some way for doing theology. Since the 1960s, Wesley's followers have often referred to those four pieces as the Wesleyan Quadrilateral, but that is a little misleading, since there is nothing unique about the fact that Wesley used them. What is unique is the way Wesley combined them. The exact nature of Wesley's use of these sources and tools is something scholars continue to debate, but the general nature of his intuitions is clear enough for us to see how we can benefit from doing theology today the way Wesley did it. We will, thus, spend the rest of this chapter looking at those pieces and the way Wesley brought them together.

Scripture

Without question, the most important element in Wesley's theological method is Scripture, but he was not born with a Bible in his hand. Like everyone else, he was introduced to Scripture by his tradition, and we will explore the significance of that recognition below. However, beginning in 1725, as a young man pursuing ordination, and more earnestly in 1730, as a fellow at Oxford, Wesley decided that Scripture had to have the primary place in his life if he wanted to follow God and God's plan of salvation.[2]

Wesley's stated motivations for putting Scripture first already show some of his theological commitments, ones we will explore in later chapters. As he says in the preface to his first volume of sermons:

I am a creature of a day, passing through life as an arrow through the air. . . . I drop into an unchangeable eternity! I want to know one thing, the way to heaven—how to land safe on that happy shore. God himself has condescended to teach the way: for this very end he came from heaven. He hath written it down in a book. O give me that book! At any price give me the Book of God! I have it. Here is knowledge enough for me. Let me be *homo unius libri* [A man of one book].[3]

Wesley's primary concern here is salvation, and he is convinced that Scripture contains the information necessary for pursuing that goal. While Wesley does not doubt that the Bible has things to say about science or history, that is not why he reads the book. His orientation to Scripture flows from his commitment to follow God's way of salvation, and it is never divorced from that. The priority here is important for understanding Wesley. Wesley does not believe in salvation because he believes in the Bible; he believes in the Bible because he is committed to listening to what is being said by the God who is saving him. This focus keeps Wesley on task, we might say, and he tries not to waste time on biblical speculations that do not affect how we live our lives with God.

In this quote we can also hear Wesley's belief in a God who communicates what God wants people to know. Wesley believes that we have no way of knowing the "way to heaven" on our own if God does not show us. Our own reason and our own experience cannot give us knowledge of God and God's world.

God has to reveal that to us. Scripture is, therefore, supremely important because it is our only source for knowing God.

This perspective on Scripture as a "revelation for salvation" is the starting point for Wesley's theology. All that he discovered and rediscovered about salvation and the Christian life, he found by looking through the lens of Scripture. If someone used Scripture in ways that hurt people's ability to connect to God, that was an abuse and misunderstanding of Scripture. Wesley's careful focus on Scripture's saving role above all else finds its way into many of the doctrinal statements on Scripture in churches that own his legacy.[4]

Wesley's commitment to Scripture was not just an academic matter; it was a central feature of his entire life. Virtually every diary entry we have from him includes time devoted to Scripture reading. His standard form of public address was the sermon. His *Journal*, his letters, and his essays are full of the words and phrases of the standard translation of Scripture used in Wesley's day (the King James Version). Wesley lived with this book, and it shaped who he was as well as what he thought. If we took Scripture away from Wesley's theology, there would be almost nothing left.

Tradition

Scripture becomes the most important thing to Wesley, but only because he belonged to a tradition that helped him to see its importance. We can think of tradition as all of the wrestling with Scripture and life that people who lived before us have passed down to us, either in person or in writing. Those traditions mean that none of us starts from scratch, but not all tradition has the same value. Some tradition is good and points us to the right road. Some tradition, however, serves better as a reminder of where the dead ends are. Wesley used tradition in a careful and nuanced way that acknowledged both its value and its danger. In this, he provides us a workable model of what critical faithfulness to tradition might look like.

As we have seen, Wesley's family gave him a broad introduction to the various traditions of Reformed Protestantism. As a good Protestant, Wesley respected tradition but never gave it the final word—that belonged to Scripture alone. If he believed a tradition contradicted his best understanding of Scripture, then he was happy to critique or reject that tradition. However, if it did not, then he was also happy to accept it and use it. He was neither bound by tradition nor a rebel against it. It was, for him, a tool. It could serve as a reference point to test different interpretations of Scripture and their application to everyday life. It gave him a place to start and a place to go so that he did not feel as though he was struggling with Scripture or with ministry alone. In Wesley's vision of theology, tradition is important but not ultimate. It helps us see things in Scripture and apply them to our lives. Without it, we might not know where to begin, but that does not mean it always tells us where to go. For Wesley, tradition was a servant of Scripture and of the lived Christian life, something to be called on when it helped and set aside when it hindered.

Wesley's attitude of critical faithfulness toward tradition can be seen in the way he used the various traditions to which he was exposed. He was, naturally, biased toward his own Anglican tradition, though he was shamelessly critical of it when he felt it violated Scripture or was not doing its job of connecting people to God. He also appreciated the tradition of German Pietism and its emphasis on the spiritual life, though he thought some of the Moravians overly spiritualized things. Finally, Wesley gave special attention to the early church fathers, particularly those who shared the Roman world of the New Testament. Since they were close to the events of Scripture and shared the poverty and persecution of the earliest church, Wesley found their reflections on faith and Scripture particularly important. However, once Constantine came to power in the early 300s and started giving status and wealth to the church, tradition became tainted and needed to be approached more critically. At the end of his life, Wesley feared the same thing was happening to his own Methodist tradition as well.

Even with that warning, however, Wesley found many writings and testimonies from the whole history of the church to be helpful and useful for understanding Scripture and for living the Christian life. The works of his *Christian Library* show that he was interested in introducing his people to a wide range of tradition, though he still carefully purged those sources of anything that he felt violated Scripture or reason or that might impede Christian experience. And so we find Wesley being faithful to tradition where he could be but critical where he had to be, and in that he set us an example still worth studying today.

Reason

Reason holds a special place, alongside Scripture, in Wesley's theological method. In fact, his normal way of defining "good theology" was theology that was both scriptural and rational. As he did with Scripture, Wesley trusted reason completely—though, also like Scripture, he did not trust everyone's use of it. For Wesley, reason was primarily a processing tool, and it took some training to learn how to properly connect known truths to one another and to use reason to open ourselves to new truth. Seeing reason as a tool also meant that Wesley did not use reason as a source for theology, since whatever material reason worked with had to come from some other place. Understanding how Wesley viewed reason and its connection to experience is important for understanding both his theological method and his theology itself.

Wesley studied at Oxford at a time when the influence of the ancient Greek thinker Aristotle was particularly strong, and he adopted Aristotle's philosophical approach. When Wesley said something was "rational," what he usually meant is that it followed the rules of proper thinking, rules that Aristotle identified as "logic." For Aristotle and for Wesley, logic gave thinking a set of objective markers, a way of determining truth that did not depend on subjective intuitions or feelings. Reason, then, was Wesley's tool for showing what was and was not true by showing how it did or did not fit in with other things that were affirmed as true.

The objective reliability of logic—particularly as a counterweight to sometimes misleading emotions—was important to Wesley and to his theology. In his own writings and sermons, Wesley was always careful to make logical connections between his ideas and not just offer metaphorical illustrations or play clever rhetorical tricks. When he analyzed the writings of others, one of his favorite things to do was to put their claims in logical form and then to show how they were built on bad assumptions or how they proceeded from faulty reasoning. Wesley was so committed to the rules of proper thinking that he even translated his own university logic textbook from Latin into English so that he could teach it to his lay preachers.

This view of reason as an objective processing tool is connected to another important feature of Wesley's understanding of reason, and that is the idea that everything reason processes comes to it from the outside. "There is nothing in the mind which is not first in the senses," Wesley said, repeating a well-known summary of Aristotle's own teaching.[5] And so Wesley's view of reason is intimately connected to his view of experience, and this holds true even for our knowledge of God. As far as Wesley was concerned, human beings were born atheists, knowing only that there must be something out there that we do not know.[6] Wesley's view of reason, thus, fits nicely with the priority Wesley gives to Scripture. Since we do not start knowing anything about God, we have to learn.

That means we need a source to learn from. That means we need the Bible. No amount of reason can teach us anything about God; only Scripture can do that.

Like tradition, reason functions in theology by giving us a place to start looking at Scripture and at God's work in the world. On the one hand, we recognize a new truth when it fits in with other truths that we already know. On the other hand, we come to doubt old beliefs when they no longer fit in with all the new ones that fit so well together. But reason has to have material to work with. If you start with a mistake, even good reason may simply lead you to more mistakes. Reason only works when it has the right material to work with. For theology, reason gets its "spiritual material" from Scripture, but it gets everything else from our experience.

Experience

We now come to Wesley's most distinctive—but also most controversial—contribution to theological method. Where Wesley's Anglican colleagues and superiors would have readily affirmed the importance of Scripture, reason, and tradition, they were quite nervous about allowing experience to speak to questions about God. There were, of course, traditions that made experience the most fundamental category for doing theology, such as the Quakers and those Wesley would have called mystics. People can imagine all kinds of doctrines or practices and then justify them by saying "God told me," a claim that is nearly impossible to test or investigate. People in Wesley's day called this "enthusiasm," and it struck fear into the hearts of calm and respectable Anglicans. Bishop Butler spoke for many Anglicans when he told Wesley, "Sir, the pretending to extraordinary revelations and gifts of the Holy Ghost is a horrid thing, a very horrid thing."[7]

Wesley was sensitive to the problems created by subjective claims to divine truth, and he shared his colleagues' fear of them. He himself wrote against the problem of enthusiasm, deploring it just as much as Bishop Butler did.[8] Wesley's views of Scripture and reason meant that experience was not allowed to speak "on its own." Subjective claims had to be tested against those objective authorities. However, Wesley believed that to give up personal experience was to give up Christianity. Wesley felt that God did act in the lives of individuals in a way that they could feel and that, in some way, this was one of the main goals of Christianity. In the preface to his sermons, he said that he wanted "to describe the true, the scriptural, experimental religion," something he later calls "heart-religion."[9] A Christianity that could not be experienced was, in Wesley's view, not the Christianity of the Bible.

However, Wesley's view of experience extends far beyond the things we normally label as inward or personal religious experience. His theology was about a God who made a difference in the physical, workaday world. It was, therefore, always important for him to test his interpretations of Scripture in the world of our sensory experience to see if they worked. And if they didn't work, Wesley said he was willing to give them up. In speaking about entire sanctification, Wesley wrote, "If I were convinced that none in England had attained what has been so clearly and strongly preached by such a number of preachers, in so many places, and for so long a time, I should be clearly convinced that we had all mistaken the meaning of those Scriptures. And therefore, for the time to come, I too must teach that 'sin will remain till death.'"[10]

Experience in Wesley's theological method was, in one sense, the goal of theology. However, it was also the crucible in which one could see if all this fancy talk about God made any real difference. Wesley believed that experience could not teach anyone anything about God apart from the Bible, but people do not know if they have understood the Bible properly until it makes a difference in the world. As we noted above, Wesley's theology was practical and focused on God's saving work in the world. The way he deals with experience in his theology anchors this approach.

These, then, are the basic pieces of Wesley's theological method. Scripture serves as the source of everything we can know about a God who is beyond this world but reveals God's self in the world. Tradition helps us by introducing us to a history of thinking about God and showing us both good and bad examples of that process. Reason teaches us to think carefully and objectively and to make sure that everything we say fits in with everything else we say. Finally, experience provides us both a goal for all this theologizing and a way to test what we say for its practical value. In balancing these four pieces together, Wesley found a way of doing theology that worked well in his world and could work equally well in ours. However, Wesley did not set out to write a theology manual. He set out to preach the gospel. Now that we have an introduction to the *how* of his theology, we are ready to listen for the *what*.

nine
Wesley's Thoughts on God

*W*esley's beliefs about God are closely tied to his beliefs about salvation. Indeed, he rarely writes about God alone. Even when discussing such abstract ideas as omnipresence or eternity, Wesley usually connects them to the role they play in God's saving work in us. Even so, as we begin to lay out Wesley's thought, it is helpful to collect his basic ideas about God from their salvation-driven contexts and put them on the table independently. Seeing them this way helps us understand the other pieces of his thought better because these ideas do come first logically. Salvation is the way it is—at least as far as Wesley is concerned—because God is the way God is.

God's Transcendence

Perhaps Wesley's most basic assumption about God is God's otherness, or "transcendence," to use the normal theological word. Most of what he says about God is rooted in the intuition that God is not like us. Though God is active in the world, God is not a part of the world. The first thing that means for Wesley—a point we touched on in the last chapter—is that God can only be known to the extent that God reveals God's self. Wesley also points to God's otherness by discussing God's spiritual nature, God's eternal nature, and that God is all-present (omnipresent), all-knowing (omniscient), and all-powerful (omnipotent). Most of those ideas are ones he shares with the large majority of theologians, but Wesley's thoughts on God's power are different from the standard view in Reformed Protestantism. We will look at each of these divine characteristics in turn.

God as Unknowable

We begin with the implication that God's transcendence makes God unknowable because how we handle that intuition shapes everything else we might claim to "know" about God. In his short list of divine attributes in the sermon "The Unity of the Divine Being," Wesley starts with the idea that God cannot be known except to the extent that God makes God's self known. Wesley's belief in God's transcendence gave him a dim view of our ability to know what God was like if left to our own devices. Since Wesley believes that we are born without any knowledge of God, even the idea that a spiritual world exists is only, in Wesley's words, "little more than faint conjecture"[1] if it is based on our own capacities. We human beings can only know what God is like because God has shown us through the Scriptures.

This theological conviction helps us to see why the Bible was so important to Wesley and why he never wanted to stray too far from it when talking about God. He would not even insist on using the word "Trinity" to describe God—even though he believed in it—precisely because "Trinity" is not a biblical word.[2] This makes Wesley much more of a biblical theologian than a systematic one. He cares about putting together the various confessions the Bible makes about God so that they make sense, but he cares more about being true to Scripture than he does about being coherent. When the pieces don't fit, Wesley tends to affirm his faith in the mysteries that Scripture reveals more than he tries to speculate about how they could be made to fit together. This is especially true when such speculation might rest more on philosophy than on biblical revelation.

What that means for readers of Wesley is that we have to accept some ambiguity in his confessions about God. Where modern readers might feel a tension, say, between Wesley's views of God's omniscience and Wesley's views on human freedom, Wesley simply affirms them both because he feels Scripture affirms them both. He offers a traditional "Arminian" view of omniscience (see below), but he does not probe it very deeply. However, while these things should concern us when we apply Wesley's thought to today, they do not need to concern us as we explore his thought back then. For now, we will simply describe Wesley's views, though we do so knowing that this leaves the job of being a good "Wesleyan" today only half finished.

God as Spirit

One of the important ways that Wesley understands God's otherness is with the confession that "God is a Spirit" (John 4:24, KJV). Wesley refers to that scripture in many sermons, and he always uses it to draw a distinction between God and God's creation, and especially between worship that is worthy of God and worship that is material or "outward" only. In fact, "pure spirituality" is, for Wesley, a uniquely divine characteristic. He seems to think that even angels have some kind of material body (that is, created nature), however refined it might be.[3]

Wesley's idea of God's spiritual nature also connects to classical affirmations of God's simplicity. This means that God is not composed of parts, as material bodies always are. Whatever God is, it cannot be broken down into something more basic than "God-ness." It also means that God is not, *by nature*, subject to the influences of the material world. Human beings are subject to "passions," involuntary biological reactions to the material world around us. Not so with God. Wesley would affirm the classical interpretation of the first of the Thirty-Nine Articles of the Church of England, which affirms that God is "without body, parts or passions." For Wesley, this does not mean God does not love us—quite the contrary! It just means that God's spiritual, simple, voluntary love is not the same thing as the physical, complex, and involuntary feeling of passion that human beings experience.

God as Eternal

God's spiritual nature means that God does not occupy material space in the way that God's creatures do. Likewise, God's eternal nature means that God does not occupy time the same way we do either. In his sermon "On Eternity," Wesley defines eternity as "boundless duration," a succession of moments that stretches out infinitely from the present moment into the past and into the future. God is the only reality to occupy all of these moments. While God will grant to creation a "boundless duration" into the future, only God has no beginning. This is another defining characteristic of God's otherness as far as Wesley is concerned. If anything else were to have always existed, it, too, would have to be God. This is why Wesley rejects the idea that matter has always existed.[4]

Wesley, however, has another idea of eternity that shows up in his works, namely the idea that God's eternity means that God stands outside of time completely and sees all time—past, present, and future—as one unified whole. This idea is more closely connected to Greek philosophy, and Wesley uses it specifically to address the question of predestination.[5] As we will see, Wesley wants to affirm that God knows the future without affirming that God causes that future. Placing God outside of time allows him to do that. Thus, talking about "foreknowledge" is a human way of speaking because for God there is no before or after, just "now."

It does not take much thought to see that these two concepts of eternity do not fit together, and there is some scholarly debate about which concept is more important to Wesley. In Wesley's concern to be biblical, at least as he sees it, he does not attempt to reconcile these competing interpretations of the relationship of God to time. However, what is consistent between them both is that, unlike us, God is not subject to time, either because God occupies it fully or because God stands outside of it. What's important, again, is God's otherness. Where we are bound by time, God is not.

The "Omni" Doctrines

God's unbounded relationship to time and space naturally leads to Wesley's appreciation of what are sometimes called the "omni" doctrines: God's omnipresence, omniscience, and omnipotence. One could treat these ideas separately, but in Wesley they seem to fit closely together. These interconnected affirmations express God's otherness, but they also imply something about the way God works in and through the world—God's immanence, in other words. We will start with Wesley's understanding of omnipresence, since that is the least controversial, before moving on to his ideas of God's omniscience and omnipotence. Those last two show Wesley's theological distance from the majority opinions of Reformed Protestantism, though they are in line with the Arminian impulses within his own Anglican tradition.

Omnipresence. This is the only "omni" doctrine that Wesley treats with focused attention, preaching a whole sermon on the subject near the end of his life (1788).[6] In this sermon, which represents the intuitions Wesley held throughout his life, Wesley defines the idea of omnipresence as simply "unbounded presence," with analogy to God's eternity and omnipotence (as "unbounded power"). Drawing from Jeremiah 23 and Psalm 139, Wesley simply affirms that God is in *this* place (wherever *this* is) and in every place, even those "places" that may be beyond the bounds of creation. Wesley uses the idea to emphasize the unequal relationship between God and God's creation, reinforcing once again God's independence and otherness. Where God exceeds creation and can exist without it, creation would collapse into nothingness if God were to withdraw God's sustaining presence.

In that sermon, Wesley also ties omnipotence to omnipresence, since he claims that God cannot act where God is not present. Elsewhere Wesley will link omniscience with omnipresence, claiming that God knows all things because God is present to all things.[7] Wesley, however, is not content with these formal speculations. The real point of talking about omnipresence for Wesley is its consequence for how we live. If God is everywhere, then that should induce us to behave in ways pleasing to God. And if we behave in ways pleasing to God, God is sure to support us wherever we are.

Omniscience. Like most Christians in his day, Wesley affirmed the idea that God is all knowing. Wesley could not conceive that God could be ignorant of anything. On that point at least, Wesley and his Calvinist opponents could all agree. However, they disagreed on the source of God's knowledge, and that disagreement is important. Most Calvinists thought God's knowledge derived from God's power and God's activity. For them, God's all-powerful-ness meant that God was the ultimate cause of everything, and God naturally knows what God caused. God knows things because God has already decided and implemented them. In a sense, they *are* because God knows them. This chain of reasoning makes God the ultimate source of God's knowledge. As we saw above, Wesley roots God's knowledge in God's omnipresence, not God's omnipotence, and that makes all the difference in the world.

To Wesley, God knows every part of God's creation because God is present to it, not because God caused it to be this way. God, thus, "sees and knows."[8] The striking difference here is that creation—not God—is then the source of God's knowledge. Wesley puts it this way in his sermon "On Predestination": "We must not think they *are* because he *knows* them. No; he knows them because they *are*."[9] Although the difference is small, its significance is radical, and it begins to speak to the kind of connection that this God-Who-Is-Other has to the world God created. The reason for this shift is that Wesley believes that God created human beings with freedom, something we will explore more deeply in the next chapter. Because human beings have freedom, they, too, can "cause" things to happen. God knows those things because God sees what these human beings have caused. Of course, God's omniscience is still a feature of God's otherness, since none of God's creatures possess that quality nor can we even completely understand it. However, by linking God's knowledge to God's creation, Wesley has hinted at a relationship between God and creation that is two-way (between God and the world) and not just one-way (from God to the world). This already sets us up for the important role that relationships will play for the rest of Wesley's theology.

Omnipotence. The bilateral relationship that is implied by Wesley's understanding of God's omniscience is fully expressed in his understanding of God's omnipotence. Wesley had to deal with the concept of omnipotence more often than he did the other two "omni" doctrines because of his debates with the Calvinists and their views on the role of God's power in salvation. We will return to the ideas of salvation later, but for now it is important to see that Wesley's understanding of God's almighty power was shaped by Wesley's understanding of what God did with that power. In other words, God only uses God's power for specific purposes. Once God has decided what God wants, God will only use power in ways consistent with those purposes. Therefore, even though Wesley affirms that God is all-powerful, he will also affirm that there are things God cannot do.

Wesley explores this idea in his sermon "On Divine Providence." There, Wesley does two things that show that he understands God's power differently from his Calvinist opponents. First, Wesley links God's power to God's wisdom and goodness. God is good and so will only do good things. Also, God is wise and so knows what is best for God's creation. Theoretical speculations about what God *could* do have no place in Wesley's world. Scripture tells us what God has done and gives us expectations about what God will do, and all those things point to a God whose power is never separated from wisdom and goodness.

The second thing that Wesley does to "limit" God's omnipotence is to argue strongly for God's "self-consistency." What God does on one occasion will be consistent with what God does on any other occasion. The means God uses are consistent with the ends God wants. Wesley says it like this: "Only he that can do all things else cannot deny himself; he cannot counteract himself, or oppose his own work."[10] This is why God does not destroy sin and evil. Though God has the power to do it, God "cannot," because that would contradict God's earlier work of creating human beings with freedom. Wesley's argument on the matter is worth quoting at length, because it is the clearest expression of the difference between his conception of omnipotence and that of his Calvinist opponents.

> For he [God] created man in his own image: a spirit, like himself; a spirit endued with understanding, with will, or affections, and liberty—without which neither his understanding nor his affections could have been any use,

neither would he have been capable either of vice or virtue. . . . Were human liberty taken away men would be as incapable of virtue as stones. Therefore (with reverence be it spoken) the Almighty himself cannot do this thing. He cannot thus contradict himself, or undo what he has done. He cannot destroy out of the soul of man that image of himself wherein he made him.[11]

We will return to the point of human freedom later, but for now we can see that Wesley's view of God's power is not that of an arbitrary tyrant. Of course, the limits on God's power are the ones that God accepts, or the ones within which God chooses to operate. So God's independence, freedom, and otherness are still important. None of God's creatures can constrain God's activity, but it seems that God can.

Holiness, Goodness, and Love

Perhaps the word that best captures Wesley's concern for God's otherness or transcendence is the word "holy." The idea that God is holy means that God is not like us, above and beyond us, separate. For Wesley, however, God's holiness always also has a moral quality. One could imagine a god that is separate in a way that had nothing to do with morality, and Wesley feels that some Calvinists do this at times.[12] For Wesley, however, God's otherness, God's holiness, cannot be separated from God's goodness. This is why Wesley most often uses the word "holy" to contrast God with the fallen and sinful state of the world. This is also why he resists talk about the "glory of God" being linked merely to great exercises of God's power. Wesley's understanding of God's glory is always linked to the manifestation of God's goodness or, to put it more in Wesley's terms, God's love.[13]

With that idea, we are brought full circle. The starting point for Wesley's thoughts about God is God's otherness, God's transcendence, God's distance from us. The ending point, however, is God's closeness, God's immanence, God's love. A God who is only a holy, omnipotent, omniscient, omnipresent, eternal, spiritual Other would be completely unknown to us. The only reason we know anything about this God is that God is also a God of love, a God who does not stay in the "great beyond" but engages the world—first by creating it, then by always sustaining it, governing it, and redeeming it.

In some sense, it is Wesley's very idea of God that *is* the gospel message. The God who is beyond us is a God of love. "Love," Wesley says, "existed from eternity, in God, the great ocean of love."[14] In fact, as far as Wesley is concerned, love is God's "reigning attribute, the attribute that sheds an amiable glory on all his other perfections."[15] God is all-powerful, but God's power is expressed in love. God is just, but God's justice is grounded in love. God is holy, but our experience of God's holiness is an experience of holy love.

God and the World

It is out of this dynamic synthesis of God's apartness and God's closeness, God's transcendence and God's immanence, that Wesley reflects on God's relationship to the world. This is why Wesley prefers the familial metaphor of God as Father over the political metaphor of God as King. He never wants to separate God's powerful activity in the world from God's loving care for the world. That loving care is expressed in three fundamental ways. First, God creates the world, and the world always remains dependent on God's sustaining power. Second, God governs the world, always interacting with it and overseeing its activity. This is what Wesley understands as God's providence. Third, God is always involved in redeeming God's fallen creation. Since the bulk of Wesley's thought—and so the rest of this book—is involved in that third idea, we will confine ourselves here to briefly exploring only those first two.

The Father God as Creator/Sustainer

Few in Wesley's eighteenth century would have doubted that God was the Creator of all things. Most took for granted that God created the world and that the Genesis account gave a historical record of that six-day process. As a firm believer in the Bible, Wesley did not question that. Scientific questions about the origin of the world had not been raised yet. When it comes to science and creation, then, we simply do not know how Wesley would have balanced his faith in the Scripture with his belief that Scripture had to be tested in our experience. However, issues of science aside, Wesley makes some claims about God through his reflections on God as Creator, claims that are important no matter how one reads the Genesis text.

First of all, Wesley says that God's relationship to the world as Creator is a strictly one-way relationship, with everything depending on God. "The eternal, almighty, all-wise, all-gracious God, is the Creator of heaven and earth. He called out of nothing by his all-powerful word the whole universe, all that is."[16] Wesley holds the classical idea of creation out of nothing (*creatio ex nihilo*), which preserves God's ultimate priority above—and independence from—the world. God has complete liberty in creation, and in Wesley's commentary on Genesis, this is one of the things that catches his attention: "So that in six days God made the world. We are not to think but that God could have made the world in an instant: but he did it in six days, that he might shew himself a free agent, doing his own work, both in his own way, and in his own time; that his wisdom, power and goodness, might appear to us, and be meditated upon by us, the more distinctly."[17]

As far as Wesley is concerned, God is not compelled to create, nor does the act of creation somehow flow spontaneously from God's nature. The act of creation is an expression of God's love, but it is a deliberate act, undertaken in a way that demonstrates to us the complete freedom of the Actor. As we will see, God's freedom is important to Wesley as the fundamental anchor for our human freedom.

Second, Wesley sees creation from the outset as an arena of love, a place where God can display God's love and empower creation—particularly in humanity—to love God back. God's purposes in creation cannot be separated, then, from God's love, and Wesley will tie together God's gifts of existence and of the ability to love. "Love had a place in all the children of God, from the moment of their creation. They received at once from their gracious Creator to exist, and to love,"[18] Wesley says in one place. Using an analogy with the sun, he says in another, "As light and heat were not subsequent to the creation of the sun, but began to exist with it, so that the moment it existed it shone; so spiritual light and heat, knowledge and love, were not subsequent to the creation of man, but they began to exist together with him. The moment he existed, he knew and loved."[19]

We will say more about this capacity for response, this "response-ability," when we look at creation and humanity in the next chapter, but it is important to note here for what it says about God. God is almighty and *could have* created a world in which every event was dictated by God. But that's not what God did, according to Wesley. Instead, God created a world that is capable of its own response, a world with which God chooses to *inter*act rather than simply control.

Part of what this meant for Wesley is that the Creator's work was not finished with the act of creation. Some in Wesley's day would have argued for a God who created the world as a grand Watchmaker. God made it, wound it up, and then left it alone to run on its own. Such a view of God's once-and-done creative activity is usually labeled deism, and it implied that the world was more or less independent of God once it had been created. That, for Wesley, was taking the world's independence too far. God gave the world "response-ability," the ability to respond to God, which is different from the ability to just do whatever it desired. Wesley rejected a deist view and insisted that the world always remains dependent on God's continuous upholding for its very existence.

> He [God] "beareth," upholdeth, sustaineth, "all" created "things by the word of his power" [Heb 1:3], by the same powerful word which brought them out of nothing. As this was absolutely necessary for the beginning of their existence, it is equally so for the continuance of it: were his almighty influence withdrawn they could not subsist a moment longer. . . . were he to withdraw his hand for a moment the creation would fall into nothing.[20]

Just as God is the only source of existence, so, too, is God also the only source of "motion" or action, the only reason why things can "happen." All other motion or power in the world derives from God. When discussing human procreation, for example, Wesley notes:

> "God is the maker of every man who comes into the world." For it is God alone who gives man power to propagate his species. Or rather, it is God himself who does the work, by man as an instrument. . . . God is really the producer of every man, every animal, every vegetable in the world; as he is the true *primum mobile*, the spring of all motion throughout the universe.[21]

It is God's continuous action that makes all creaturely action possible, but again, we should remind ourselves that what God makes possible is response. Wesley even used the idea of God's constant action in the world to counter the claim that everything in the world—even human activity—was dictated by the deterministic forces of nature. He figures that God can intervene in the human body and brain to create our freedom and not leave us subject to those forces.[22] So, for Wesley, it might even be true in a physical, as well as spiritual, sense that without God's action our free response would be impossible.

Now, as Wesley will immediately go on to argue, this does not mean that God "causes" all things. To use a distinction from Wesley's treasured logic, God's action is *necessary* for anything to happen, but it is not *sufficient*. God's agency makes other agents possible, but they must actualize the possibilities God gives them for themselves. When they do that, they assume responsibility for what they do with the power that God gives them. How God deals with the other active agents in the world takes us away from God's unilateral role as Creator and Sustainer into God's relational role as Governor.

Providence and the Father God as Governor

God's creating and sustaining power provides creation with the possibility of responding to God. God's providence, then, demonstrates how God responds to creation's responses. Wesley seemed to naturally break up God's providential or governing work into two kinds: how God deals with the inanimate world and how God deals with the animate world, especially human beings. While we are more concerned with the latter, the former still helps us round out Wesley's picture of God.

Wesley sees God's interaction with the inanimate world of rocks, fire, water and the like as direct control. He does not speculate much about this, but in his mind it seems as if the so-called natural world has little independence from the divine will. As we saw above, Wesley believed that God was constantly acting on the world, and so he tended not to make a distinction between "natural events" and ones that God caused. For Wesley, there was little tension between natural and divine causes, since what we call nature is simply our observation of God's normal pattern of activity on the world. "What is nature itself," Wesley writes, "but the art of God, or God's method of acting in the material world?"[23] While that close connection raises questions about "natural evil," Wesley does not seem to worry about that. His concern is to emphasize God's freedom over the world. While he shares his culture's scientific assumptions about the regularity of the world, he insists that God is always free to interrupt God's normal pattern of activity. Wesley was, thus, committed to the idea that there were miracles, places where God's activity became obvious. Given his focus on salvation, Wesley preferred to talk about the "miracles of grace"—things such as conversions and transformed lives[24]—more than about miraculous healings or unexplainable events. However, he did affirm those things and comment on them in his *Journal* when he encountered them.

Wesley's view of God's interaction with human beings is much more significant than his view of God's work through nature. Here Wesley emphasizes God's respect for human freedom as God moves the world toward God's ultimate design. For Wesley, the trait that best articulates this balancing act is divine wisdom. If God were to just impose God's will on the world, "it would imply no wisdom at all, but barely a stroke of omnipotence. Whereas all the manifold wisdom of God (as well as all his power and goodness) is displayed in governing man as man; not as a stock or a stone, but as an intelligent and free spirit, capable of choosing either good or evil. Herein appears the depth of the wisdom of God in his adorable providence!"[25]

God is always at work in creation to provide humanity with "every possible help" so that humans can choose good and turn away from evil.[26] The God of love is constantly acting to secure the best for those creatures God created in God's image. But God is, at least in Wesley's eyes, committed to only work *with* the liberty God created and not to override it. That God can do this and still achieve the ultimate ends God desires gives us a better reason to glorify God than merely seeing God demonstrate God's power.

Because God responds to human beings as they respond to God, Wesley promotes the idea of "circles" or levels of divine providence (which he got from the seventeenth-century Puritan Thomas Crane).[27] In his sermon "On Divine Providence," Wesley articulates three circles. The first is the one that contains all of humanity. God acts in love toward everyone because, as Wesley notes, "His love is not confined."[28] That said, Wesley still believes that God takes a more immediate care over those who are Christian, because they have responded to God more fully. Finally, there is the circle of God's most intimate care, the circle of those who have wholeheartedly given themselves to God and God's work, who worship God "in spirit and in truth," and who walk as Christ himself walked. Wesley does not explain what this means in detail, but it is consistent with the picture of God he paints throughout his works. If God responds to the responses of God's creatures, it makes sense that the depth of God's responses would correspond to the depth of theirs. And Wesley will use this point to encourage his hearers and readers to respond all the more deeply to God, that God may respond all the more deeply to them.

Trinity

Before we move on from Wesley's thoughts about God, we have to cover one more traditional doctrine that connects the issues of God's transcendence, God's immanence, and God's interaction with the world. That is the doctrine of the Trinity. Wesley's understanding and use of the doctrine of the Trinity is a matter of some scholarly debate. Some people claim that Wesley's doctrine of God is thoroughly Trinitarian, while others say that the doctrine as a concept was not that important to him. It is not our place here to solve this debate but rather to show the tensions in Wesley's use of the Trinity that have caused it to arise.

On the one hand, Wesley clearly acknowledges and owns the doctrine. He will at times explicitly refer to the Christian God as the three-in-one God, and he preaches on explicitly Trinitarian texts. Though he only published one sermon on the topic, in that sermon he clearly stated that belief in the Trinity was one of the most important beliefs of the Christian faith.[29] In addition, Wesley has a well-developed idea of the Holy Spirit, and that would be impossible without the foundation that the doctrine of the Trinity lays. These things would suggest that the Trinity was important to Wesley.

On the other hand, once we move beyond the strong affirmation of the doctrine in Wesley, there is little else to talk about. Wesley shies away from exploring the idea theologically, even to the point of condemning attempts to understand it. It does not come up as a topic in his writings, and that one sermon he did publish was printed in 1775, rather late in his career. Even there, in a sermon devoted to the Trinity, Wesley makes no attempt to explain what the Trinity means or how it connects to the life of faith. Instead, he helps his readers see that they can, indeed, believe something that they do not comprehend. He claims that all God requires of them is to admit the Trinity as a fact, not to explain how God's nature works.

One way to hold together this odd combination of affirmation and neglect is to see the doctrine of the Trinity as playing an important but implicit role in Wesley's thought, one that he himself might not have fully appreciated. As Albert Outler puts it, "For Wesley, as for pietists generally, abstruse [i.e., hard to understand] doctrines are better believed devoutly than analysed rationally."[30] Even though Wesley does not explicitly use the doctrine of the three-in-one God as a meaningful theological concept, Wesley's thought fits together better if its implicit Trinitarian foundation is recognized. This is particularly true when considering the priority of love in Wesley's conception of God, since the Trinity—especially as understood by the early Eastern fathers—shows how God can *be* love, how the word "God" refers, in a sense, to a loving community of Father, Son, and Holy Spirit. Here, again, we should remind ourselves that Wesley was a practical theologian. Rightly or wrongly, he saw little practical implication for the doctrine of the Trinity, and so he gave it little attention. However, given everything else that Wesley says about God, the doctrine of the Trinity can still serve the practical purpose of tying together various strands of his thought.

This, then, is a summary of the major points of Wesley's thought about God. As we have already emphasized, Wesley's primary theological concern was the great drama of salvation, and God is unquestionably the primary Actor in that drama. However, before we engage that drama directly, we must first explore a few of Wesley's basic ideas about creation as the stage on which that drama unfolds and about human beings as the drama's secondary—but still important—actors.

ten

Wesley's Thoughts on Creation and Humanity

The way Wesley understands creation and the original state of humanity grounds his understanding of sin and salvation. He understood salvation as a kind of restoration, a "new creation" that brings God's created order back on track after having been derailed by sin. So, we need to know what that track looked like before sin messed everything up. Like most Christians of his day, Wesley saw human beings as the primary targets of God's saving work, but unlike many Christians he was clear that salvation encompassed everything else as well. Seeing how Wesley understood the original state of creation helps us appreciate what God does when God saves, redeems, and restores it.

In this chapter, then, we will take a quick look at two basic intuitions Wesley had about creation in general before focusing more of our attention on his views of "original humanity." Wesley saw creation as good and that in a relational and dynamic way. He also believed that creation consisted of two parts that are separate in principle but always integrated in practice—the spiritual and the physical. After exploring those intuitions, we will look at Wesley's thoughts on original humanity. Wesley understands our original nature as rooted in the idea that we were created in God's image, but he also sees in that nature a unique combination of the spiritual and physical forces that he feels govern all of creation. These glimpses into original creation and original humanity will give us the background we need to appreciate Wesley's view of what goes wrong when the corrupting force of sin enters the world.

Creation

Wesley had a very high view of creation, higher than probably most of the Christians of his day. Many people looked at this fallen and broken world as something humans needed to be saved from. Wesley, on the other hand, saw the whole world—not just human beings—as the focus of God's redemptive activity. To Wesley, God is not interested in helping people escape the world but rather wants people to participate in its redemption. There are two intuitions he had on creation that help us to make sense of this approach to salvation: the idea that the goodness of creation was a dynamic and relational reality, and the idea that creation has two distinct but intertwined facets. We will look a bit more deeply at each of these intuitions in turn.

Creation as Dynamically Good

Perhaps the most important intuition Wesley has about creation is that it is good, and this goodness is understood as a dynamic and relational reality. In this, we see the clear priority of Scripture as a source for Wesley's intuitions over experience. Some people are tempted to doubt God's goodness—if not God's very existence—because they see a much-less-than-perfect world around them. While Wesley would not deny that the world we live in contains much evil, he felt it was a mistake to evaluate creation by starting with our present experience of it. That experience is tainted by sin. If we want to understand creation, we must go to Scripture, and Scripture—at least in Wesley's eyes—links up the goodness of creation with the goodness of its Creator.

> All things then, without exception, were very good. And how should they be otherwise? There was no defect at all in the power of God, any more than in his goodness or wisdom. . . . "As for God, his way is perfect" [2 Sam. 22:31]—and such originally were all his works. And such they will be again, when "the Son of God" shall have "destroyed all the works of the devil" [1 John 3:8].[1]

Wesley's belief in the original goodness of creation is, thus, grounded both in biblical testimony (from Gen. 1) and in the theological link between the character of God and the character of God's creative work. Notice, too, how Wesley uses the original goodness of creation to point toward the eventual goodness it will have once God finishes God's redeeming work.

This link is important because many people felt that the fall had completely erased all original goodness from creation. On this view, God's salvation means that God has to start over, since there really isn't anything good left in creation worth saving. Human beings—even the physical world itself—have become so evil that they are worthy only of punishment and destruction. Salvation may be extended to a few people to whom God will show grace, but the rest of creation is doomed, and deservedly so.

Wesley did not think that way. He believed that salvation was new creation, but he affirmed that new creation was built on original creation. The fall damaged creation so that it no longer functions as God created it to function, but that is different from an irretrievable loss of goodness. To Wesley, God's work of redemption is more like a healing that restores health; it is not an arbitrary choice to exempt some small part of creation from its just punishment.

Wesley can have this view because his idea of goodness is not the idea of some "thing" that can be lost. Rather, the goodness of creation is found in the dynamic interrelationship between all the things God made and in the relationship that the whole of creation has with God. Wesley offers this view in his sermon on Genesis 1:31, called "God's Approbation of His Works." There Wesley writes,

> Whatever was created was good in its kind, suited to the end for which it was designed, adapted to promote the good of the whole and the glory of the great Creator. This sentence it pleased God to pass with regard to each particular creature. But there is a remarkable variation of the expression with regard to all the parts of the universe taken in connexion with each other, and constituting one system: "And God saw everything that he had made; and behold, it was very good!"[2]

Goodness is, thus, a relational idea for Wesley. Like the organs in a body or the cogs in a machine, a good piece is a piece that contributes to the proper functioning of the whole. And the whole is good when it fulfills the purpose for which it was designed—which for creation is the glory of God. That's why the whole of creation can be "very good," even better than any of its pieces. This makes little sense if goodness is a static quality found in things, but it makes perfect sense if goodness is a dynamic quality found in relationships. So while the full and proper function of creation was compromised by sin, God is not interested in throwing it away and starting over. Instead, God wants to put those original pieces back together so that they function properly again.

This dynamic idea of goodness creates a tension in Wesley's thought when it comes to the idea of ultimate goodness or perfection, which is an important idea for his understanding of salvation. On the one hand, Wesley will sometimes describe God's original creation as perfect in a way that sounds static. This comes out especially in the way Wesley contrasts God's originally perfect world with the imperfect world we live in today.[3] However, there are other times in which Wesley describes God's originally perfect world as perfectly designed to get even better. For example, Wesley claimed that God made the animals with a capacity for self-improvement, meaning that their original good state could get even better.[4] More interestingly, he understands that tempting tree in the garden of Eden as something designed by God to give humanity a chance to earn even greater rewards (even though humans used it to make things worse).

"But if Adam was originally perfect in holiness" (say *perfectly holy*, made in the moral image of God), "what occasion was there for any farther trial?" That there might be room for farther holiness and happiness. Entire holiness does not exclude growth. Nor did the *right state* of all his faculties entitle him to that full reward which would have followed the *right use* of them.[5]

So, creation was perfectly good, but it seems that this means it is perfectly capable of getting even better. Wesley's idea of perfection, like his idea of goodness, is better understood as dynamic, and Wesley himself admitted that perfection had different degrees.[6] That something is as good as it can be now does not mean God cannot make it even better in the future. It is this capacity for ever greater growth and improvement that was lost in the fall, and this is what God seeks to restore in salvation. Once restored, creation will continue to improve so that the goodness of God's final salvation is going to be even better than the "perfect" goodness of God's original creation. Wesley speculates on this ultimate state of harmony in his sermon "The New Creation." There he claims that "the earth shall then be a more beautiful paradise than Adam ever saw"[7] and that human beings will enjoy "an unmixed state of holiness and happiness far superior to that which Adam enjoyed in paradise."[8]

This idea of creation as something designed by God for growth and relational goodness shapes how Wesley understands salvation in profound ways. First of all, it reminds us that all of creation fits together and that God's plan of redemption includes all of it—not just human beings. Second, it presents a positive view of the world rather than a negative or suspicious one. All sin and evil can do is delay God's plans, not ultimately frustrate them. The world, under God's command, will move in God's direction. This makes Wesley's theology a theology of hope from the very beginning. Finally, such a view of creation anchors Wesley's concern for salvation as a here-and-now reality, not something we have to wait for in some future world. There will be more in that future than there is now, certainly. But whatever God will do then is intimately connected to what God is doing even now.

Creation as Physical and Spiritual

There is another strong intuition that Wesley has about creation, and it, too, shapes his views of salvation. That is the idea that creation consists of two distinct parts—physical and spiritual. Each facet of creation has its own characteristics, but both facets always work together. We will explore the particular significance of this idea for Wesley's thoughts on human beings below, but for now we will simply touch on its significance in general.

To Wesley, the physical world is the world of our senses and the world determined by the strict laws of science. It is the world of matter, and it is essentially passive. The spiritual world consists of that part of creation that is not accessible to our senses. It is the world of angels and demons and the human soul. This is the world of activity and freedom, though it, too, has limitations. As we saw in the last chapter, only God's nature is free from all external limits, so even spiritual creation has boundaries.

We have already encountered one important implication of this division when we looked at the importance of revelation for our knowledge of the spiritual world. Given the sharp distinction between the physical and the spiritual, our ordinary way of knowing things (that is, through our senses) cannot help us with spiritual realities. Those limitations are important to Wesley, and he writes two separate sermons about them.[9] So even though Wesley has a high esteem for what we can learn through logic and through our experience, he confines their work to the physical world. To reach beyond the physical world, we need "faith," which Wesley often treats like a sense that gives us access to the spiritual world, most often through Scripture. Without faith and without the Bible, we would not even know that such a spiritual world exists.

However, while faith is necessary for those of us in the physical world to *know* the spiritual world, the two worlds are not disconnected from each other—quite the opposite. Faith simply allows us to see the truth, which is that the physical world is dependent on the spiritual, and the spiritual is mediated in and through the physical. We've already seen this in Wesley's understanding of providence and of nature as the "art of God," God at work through natural causes. In fact, Wesley will ultimately attribute *all* motion in the physical world to spiritual causes—be it through God, angels, demons or the souls of human beings. Nothing happens in the physical world unless it is acted upon by the spiritual. In fact, he says that the principle of self-motion, of originating action, is "the proper distinguishing difference between spirit and matter, which is totally, essentially passive and inactive, as appears from a thousand experiments."[10]

Wesley, then, does not share the suspicion of some that the spiritual and physical worlds are supposed to be antagonistic to one another or that the physical world is bad while only the spiritual world is good. In Wesley's mind, they form two parts of one integrated and good whole. To be sure, the spiritual world is the more important and more enduring part, but the physical world—at least when used as God intends—is designed to promote the same ideals as the spiritual world—relationship with God and between God's creatures. Sin impairs this interaction, but it does not destroy it. When seen with the eyes of faith, the physical world testifies to the existence of the spiritual. In fact, in Wesley's mind, that seems to be one of its primary functions.

One of Wesley's weightier works was his *Survey of the Wisdom of God in Creation; or, A Compendium of Natural Philosophy.* The order of the title and subtitle here is significant, as it shows Wesley's general approach to creation. Physical things may be interesting in their own right, and learning about them may be useful, but their best use is to point toward the God who made them. In this work, which Wesley heavily adapted from a Latin source, he surveys the wonders of creation, from the human body to animals, plants, fossils, the earth, and the heavens. Each section contains detailed descriptions of the parts of creation, but they are related in ways designed to point to God. In reading the work, one gets a sense that Wesley believed the world to be amazing and wonderful but that the Creator of the world was more amazing still. The world is good, but the world's goodness points to the greater goodness of the God who is behind and beyond it. As Wesley puts it:

> In short, the world around us is the mighty volume wherein God hath declared himself. Human languages and characters are different in different nations. And those of one nation are not understood by the rest. But the book of nature is written in an universal character, which every man may read in his own language. It consists not of words, but things which picture out the Divine perfections. . . .
>
>   . . . every part of nature directs us to nature's God.[11]

Elsewhere Wesley balances this appreciation of what is often called general revelation with the concern we noted above—that only special revelation or Scripture can tell you anything about God. The resulting combination means that even so-called heathens who have no access to the Scripture still have enough information and grace to know *that* there is a God. However, without Scripture, they have no way of knowing what this God is really like.

The interconnection between the physical and spiritual worlds will have implications for many other parts of Wesley's thought, such as salvation, which is a physical as well as a spiritual reality, and the work of the church, where such things as sacraments are physical forms that convey spiritual grace. However, it is most clear in that special part of creation that God made to be the primary bridge between the two worlds, and so we must now take a look at Wesley's views of humanity.

Humanity and the Image of God

Wesley's favorite shorthand for discussing the essential nature of human beings—whatever it is that makes a human being truly human—was the biblical phrase "image of God." He gets the phrase from Genesis 1:27, but for him it covers much more than what is said in that verse. He uses it to cover many things that Scripture reveals to humanity about itself. The most important of those, however, is that human beings were created for relationship with God.

The Relational Image

In his sermon "God's Approbation of His Works," Wesley retells the whole creation story, culminating with the creation of human beings. This is the highest point of God's creation because there is something special about humanity, something that sets it apart—even above—the rest of God's good creation. Human beings are "created in the image of God, and designed to know, to love, and enjoy his Creator to all eternity."[12] For Wesley, these are not two separate affirmations about humanity but two ways of saying the same thing. Human beings bear the image of God, and that means they were designed to relate to God and find their happiness in God and in God alone.

Alone of all God's creatures—all of whom are good—human beings are enough like God to be "capable of God,"[13] as Wesley puts it in another sermon. They alone are "persons" the way the three-in-one God is a God of three persons. The capacity for this relationship is the whole reason God created human beings in the first place. "Having prepared all things for him, 'He [God] created man in his own image, after his likeness.' And what was the end of his creation? It was one, and no other: that he might know, and love, and enjoy, and serve his great Creator to all eternity."[14]

Again and again, Wesley links the idea of being created in the image of God with the idea of being created for relationship with God. In another sermon, he puts it even more simply: "You were made to be happy in God."[15]

Wesley is sometimes identified as a *eudaemonist*, a fancy word for someone who believes that the chief end of human existence is happiness. For Wesley, however, the happiness for which human beings were created can only be found in a proper relationship with God. Happiness is often sought in parts of creation rather than in the Creator, but this is a futile quest. So essential is this to our true humanity that Wesley will even say that those who do not live out the image of God—who refuse to know, love, and enjoy God and find their happiness in God alone—have forsaken their true humanity and degraded themselves to the level of mere beasts.[16]

This is a simple point, but it is impossible to overemphasize its importance in Wesley's thought. At its core, Wesley's view of human nature is relational. Where some traditions might talk about human beings as instruments—tools, even—that God uses to bring glory to God's self, Wesley equates "giving glory to God" with "being happy in God."[17] The image of God stamped on human nature makes our happiness in God both possible and necessary. Our true humanity is found when we find God and lost when we lose touch with God. This image-as-relationship has been damaged by the fall, and so it is the image-as-relationship that God renews in salvation.

Wesley, however, is not content to merely affirm *that* human beings are "capable of God." He is interested in *how* this is possible. What are those features of God's nature that God shares with humanity and that enable humanity to relate back to God? Borrowing a set of ideas from Isaac Watts,[18] Wesley divides the idea of the image of God into three facets: the "natural image," the "political image," and the "moral image." We will take a brief look at each of these.

The Natural Image

For Wesley, the natural image of God in humanity consists of those spiritual capacities that make personal relationships possible, and there are three of them: understanding, will, and liberty. These are not necessarily unique to human beings—animals possess them to some degree[19] and angels and demons have them too.[20] They are, however, indispensable means by which we conduct our personal relationships with God and with others. Without them, no such relationships are possible.

In his sermon "What Is Man?" Wesley reflects a bit on humanity's embodied nature—a point to which we will return below—and then begins to explore humanity's spiritual side with these words:

> But beside this strange compound of the four elements, earth, water, air, and fire, I find something in me of a quite different nature, nothing akin to any of these. I find something in me that *thinks*. . . . Something which sees, and hears, and smells, and tastes, and feels, all which are so many modes of thinking. It goes farther: having perceived objects by any of these senses it forms inward ideas of them. It *judges* concerning them. . . . It *reasons* concerning them. . . . It *reflects* upon its own operations. It is endued with imagination and memory.[21]

This is Wesley's understanding of "understanding," something he virtually equates with Aristotle's view of reason as we encountered it earlier. This is a spiritual quality, not a physical one (matter doesn't *think*, according to Wesley), and so it is ultimately connected to the nature of God. For Wesley, the capacity for knowledge is one of the things that makes personal relationships possible. It is what marks the difference between engaging with something outside of ourselves and merely reacting to it. All kinds of creatures react to their environment, but God has given human beings the capacity to understand. This allows their encounters with others and with God to turn into relationships. In fact, Wesley seems to think that understanding pursued for its own sake—outside of the context of relating well to God and others—can easily turn into "spiritual idolatry" and end up doing more harm than good.[22]

After a few speculations on where in the physical body the spiritual feature of thinking might reside, Wesley continues his reflection as follows:

> This inward principle . . . is capable not only of thinking, but likewise of love, hatred, joy, sorrow, desire, fear, hope, etc., and a whole train of other inward emotions which are commonly called "passions" or "affections." They are styled, by a general appellation, "the will," and are mixed and diversified a thousand ways. And they seem to be the only spring of action in that inward principle I call "the soul."[23]

The "will" for Wesley is what makes us want things or want to do things. While in human beings, these emotions or desires are always physically embedded, Wesley sees the fact of desire as a spiritual inheritance, part of the image of God. It is here that Wesley locates the possibility of love in the human life, and we have already seen how central that idea is to Wesley's conception of God. Since the fall, of course, other desires have arisen that lead humanity away from right relationship with God and with other people, but this must be seen as a corruption of our human nature, not an expression of it. Human beings were given the capacity for desire so that they could love God and love their neighbor. Setting the will right, as we will see, is a good deal of what Wesley believes God's work of sanctification to be about.

The third feature of our human nature that derives from God's nature is the one that makes human beings into responsible (and response-able) persons. That is the property of freedom or liberty. In some sense, this is the linchpin of Wesley's theological anthropology, the pivot on which his entire theology turns. If humanity did not have liberty, Wesley says, "all the rest would have been in vain, and he would have been no more capable of serving his Creator than a piece of earth or marble."[24] Continuing in the sermon "What Is Man?" Wesley describes it this way:

> I am conscious to myself of one more property, commonly called *liberty*. This is very frequently confounded with the *will*, but is of a very different nature. . . . It is a power of self-determination. . . . I am full as certain of this, that I am free with respect to these, to speak or not to speak, to act or not to act, to do this or the contrary, as I am of my own existence. . . . And although I have not an absolute power over my own mind, because of the corruption of my nature, yet through the grace of God assisting me I have a power to choose and do good as well as evil. I am free to choose whom I will serve, and if I choose the better part, to continue therein even unto death.[25]

As we noted above, Wesley believed that matter was inert and that only spirit was capable of initiating action. Liberty, then, is that quality that makes this happen. Where understanding lets us know what is out there and will gives us motivation toward or away from what we know, it is liberty that exercises the choice to act.

Wesley is sensitive to the fact that many people confound liberty and will because people tend to choose what they desire. Wesley, however, enforces a distinction between them, a distinction that is important for his views on the renewal of the image of God in salvation. Liberty is influenced by understanding and by will, but it is not dominated by them. As he says in the quote, he is free to choose good or evil. Knowing the good does not always lead to doing the good, and people can know the good and still do evil because God has made them free. However, just as we are free to follow our desires, we are also free to thwart them. Liberty, therefore, is not doing whatever we want to do—that is exactly the confusion Wesley wants to avoid. Sometimes, especially in our fallen state, we want the wrong things. Wesley will compare the freedom of just doing what we want to the freedom of the devils in hell,[26] not the freedom of those created in the image of God.

Another facet of Wesley's understanding of liberty is that it is always tied to accountability, which one might expect if liberty was designed to function in relationships. It is freedom that makes us able to respond and thus responsible. We exercise our human freedom within a framework of consequences, partly established by God and partly set up by other human beings. So, for example, Wesley will argue for religious liberty in society because each person is accountable to God and God alone for the way he or she worships.[27] However, people must obey the rational laws that are set down by human society, because to exercise one's choices outside of such boundaries is not liberty but "licentiousness."[28] This idea, too, will shape the way Wesley understands our full humanity—our image of God—to be restored to us in God's work of sanctification.

One last facet of liberty's connection to the natural image of God in humanity concerns the balance between human and divine choices in the process of salvation. Wesley and his followers have always been accused by their Calvinist opponents of what is known as the Pelagian heresy. This is the belief that human beings have sufficient liberty to choose or reject God without God's help. Especially in Protestantism, this position appears to contradict the gospel message that we could do nothing to save ourselves as human beings. Everything in salvation happens by grace and by grace alone. Many feared that Wesley's attention to human liberty would compromise the work of God and make salvation a matter of human works.

Wesley fought this battle all his life. We will return to this question when we look at his views on grace, but for now we can point to Wesley's distinction between the natural image as it first appeared in Adam and the natural image we are able to recover today. According to Wesley, Adam was basically a Pelagian. He was given sufficient grace in his very creation to follow his perfect understanding and his perfect will into a perfectly obedient use of his liberty before God. He did not do so, however, and as a consequence, we no longer have his original freedom. If any liberty is restored to us, it is only through grace. That is why Wesley mentioned, in the quote on liberty above, "the grace of God assisting me." The difference between Calvin and Wesley is not a difference between grace as God's work and freedom as ours. The difference is whether God's grace accomplishes salvation on its own or restores to us sufficient freedom to cooperate. As we noted above, the liberty God originally gave to Adam and the liberty Christ restores to us is designed to function toward a particular end, and that is a proper relationship with God that results in proper relationships with other human beings and with the rest of God's created order.

The Political Image

Wesley gives less attention to the idea that human beings are created in the political image of God than he does to the natural image and the moral image, and a number of Wesley's interpreters have noted the issues that might have arisen from this neglect.[29] However, he does mention it, and it has some important implications for the way humanity relates to God and to the rest of God's creation.

Wesley uses the phrase "political image" to denote humanity's role as "governor of this lower world, having 'dominion over the fishes of the sea, and over the fowl of the air, and over the cattle, and over all the earth.'"[30] Elsewhere Wesley sums up his discussion of the image of God in humanity by pointing out that God chose to govern the created order through humanity, "So that man was God's vicegerent upon earth, the prince and governor of this lower world; and all the blessings of God flowed through him to the inferior creatures. Man was the channel of conveyance between his Creator and the whole brute creation."[31] The political image, then, refers to how human beings exercise power and how they mediate the blessings of God's spiritual rule to the rest of God's physical creation.

One implication of this is that God intends human beings to use their power the way God does. There is a difference between "dominion" and "domination." Just as God always acts toward the good of all that is under God's power, so, too, human beings were created to use their power for the good of that "lower world" of which they were made governors. In God's original and good creation, power was meant to be used in loving—rather than selfish—

ways. Wesley makes this point by means of contrast, however, since the world we live in suffers from humanity's misuse of the power entrusted to it. Because all of creation is interrelated, all of creation is impaired by humanity's failure to live out its political image of God. In particular, humanity's sin means that human beings can no longer mediate God's blessing to the rest of creation, and so all creation suffers. For now, creation is subject to the selfish desires, the "domination," of human beings, instead of benefiting from their loving attention, their "dominion." That is why the "whole creation groans" (Rom. 8:22, NKJV). However, God will even make all of this right in the final redemption of all things, and so creation hopes as well.[32]

Thus Wesley's idea of the political image of God is connected to his concept of stewardship. Wesley describes the kind of "power" human beings have "on loan" from God as the power of a "steward." Everything in this material world is only entrusted to humankind for a while so that human beings may guide everything toward God's purposes—not their own. Wesley explores this theme in detail in his sermon "The Good Steward,"[33] but it is also at work in the way he approaches ministry and parenthood.[34] God shares power with human beings, not so that they can do whatever they like, but so that they can have the chance to imitate God and work for the benefit of those under their power. Since all power is ultimately held by God, God will judge all uses of power, rewarding those who use it well and punishing those who use it poorly.

While Wesley does not explicitly tie his concerns about the political image of God in human beings to the human political order, the two still fit well together. Wesley has a dim view of democratic and republican forms of government, and he explicitly endorses the idea of a limited monarchy. Part of the reason for this has to do with the stewardship of power, which is easier to articulate in the latter case than it is in the former. It seems a very Wesleyan approach to politics to say that one should govern human beings as God does, using power only for the benefit of those entrusted to one's care.

The Moral Image

The third facet of the image of God for Wesley is the moral image. In some sense, this is the one that is most important to Wesley. Where the natural image of God deals with humanity's capacities as a reflection of God and the political image of God deals with humanity's function, the moral image deals with humanity's character, which was designed to be like God's as well. In fact, the moral image gives the proper orientation to the other two.[35] Wesley's articulation of this image is worth quoting in detail.

"And God," the three-one God, "said, Let us make man in our image, after our likeness. So God created man in his own image, in the image of God created he him" [Gen. 1:26-27]. Not barely in his *natural image* . . . nor merely in his *political image* . . . but chiefly in his *moral image*, which, according to the Apostle, is "righteousness and true holiness" [Eph. 4:24]. In this image of God was man made. "God is love": accordingly man at his creation was full of love, which was the sole principle of all his tempers, thoughts, words, and actions. God is full of justice, mercy, and truth: so was man as he came from the hands of his Creator. God is spotless purity: and so man was in the beginning pure from every sinful blot. Otherwise God could not have pronounced *him* as well as all the other work of his hands, "very good" [Gen. 1:31].[36]

This quote comes from the beginning of one of Wesley's most famous sermons on salvation, and it reveals Wesley's starting point for his approach to that topic. As we noted above, Wesley does not begin with the idea of how sinful humanity is now; he starts with the glorious creatures God created them to be. Of course, the point of the sermon is how we get back to that now that we have lost that identity through the fall and through sin, but that difference in starting point is very important.

Over and over again throughout his sermons, Wesley articulates his view of salvation and redemption as the restoration or renewal of the image of God in human beings. What God does in salvation is intimately connected to what God did in creation. As we will see in the next chapter, the tragedy of sin for Wesley entails more than the threat of future punishment because we have broken God's law. The tragedy is that we have lost our true identity, squandered our inheritance, as it were.[37] The good news, however, is that God wants to help us get that back.

We will explore Wesley's thoughts on salvation in more detail in future chapters, but it is helpful here to show how they are rooted in his intuitions about humanity. Many people feel that things such as "righteousness and holiness" are alien to human nature, foreign dispositions that would have to be imported (or imputed) from some outside source, namely God. Human nature, in this view, is fallen human nature. Whatever Adam might have been is irrelevant to us. Wesley, however, takes a different view. To him, the essence of humanity is found in being created in God's image. That means it is "natural" for human beings to reflect God's righteousness and holiness, moral goodness, mercy, justice, and the like. These qualities are not foreign to human nature; they are exactly what human nature was supposed to be. Sin is the unnatural thing. We do not sin because we are human. Rather we sin—as our first parents did—because we choose to be something less than human. Wesley's insistence on the moral image of God stamped on human nature sets up a view of salvation much larger than simply declaring one who was guilty to be innocent—however important that will be as a starting place. Salvation is nothing less than a recovery of our full humanity so that we might live as God intended, knowing, loving, enjoying, and serving our Creator.[38]

This, then, is how Wesley sees humanity as created in the image of God. We were created to live in right relationship with God, with each other, and with the rest of God's creation. To make that happen, God gave us understanding, will, and liberty (the natural image), God shared God's power with us and invited us to be stewards over all that God made (the political image), and God stamped God's very character of love, righteousness, and holiness (the moral image) on us. The tragedy of sin is that human beings degraded this image by doing things their own way. The glory of salvation is that God wants to restore this image so that it can flourish again.

Humanity as "Embodied Spirits"

While Wesley articulates most of his key ideas about what it means to be human through his concept of the image of God, there is one that Wesley treats separately. This is the idea that human beings are a unique combination of those two parts of creation we examined above—the spiritual and the physical. We are "embodied spirits," Wesley says.[39] Before we leave Wesley's view of human beings, then, we will need to explore what this means for our human nature.

The idea that we have a soul, or that we *are* a soul, seemed self-evident to Wesley. After all, we are capable of self-determination and self-motion, and purely material things cannot do this. This soul is the seat of human identity—whatever it is that makes us unique as individuals[40]—and it has been given immortality by God and so will exist into eternity.[41] These were common beliefs in Wesley's day, and so he gives little further argument for them. The interesting part of Wesley's understanding is how he sees those souls as always "embodied," and what implications that has for salvation and the spiritual life.

Wesley saw our human embodiment as simply a feature of the way God created us. Since Wesley knew that everything in the material world was good, he knew that our physical bodies were so as well.[42] He was not tempted to think that our bodies are somehow evil or that we are physical because we are fallen. He freely acknowledged that our fallen state often makes our physical nature burdensome, but that is a problem of sin for Wesley, not a problem of embodiment. Wesley believed that we would be embodied spirits even in the new creation that would last forever. "Indeed," Wesley writes, "at present this body is so intimately connected with the soul that I seem to consist of both. In my present state of existence I undoubtedly consist both of soul and body. And so I shall again after the resurrection to all eternity."[43]

This interconnectedness means that we experience the physical and spiritual facets of our existence together. Physical causes can have spiritual effects, and spiritual causes can have physical effects, and this shapes the way we approach both our physical and our spiritual life. On the one hand, our fallen nature impacts the way God's image in us can express itself. However much we might wish it otherwise, it is simply a feature of our composite existence:

And by sad experience we find, that this "corruptible body presses down the soul." It very frequently hinders the soul in its operations, and at best serves it very imperfectly. Yet the soul cannot dispense with its service, imperfect as it is. For an embodied spirit cannot form one thought but by the mediation of its bodily organs. For thinking is not (as many suppose) the act of a pure spirit, but the act of a spirit connected with a body, and playing upon a set of material keys.[44]

On the other hand, God also uses our physical nature in ways that empower our spiritual nature. Wesley preaches a whole sermon, titled "The Duty of Constant Communion," in which he encourages his hearers to receive the Lord's Supper—a very physical expression of worship—as often as they can because, in his words, "As our bodies are strengthened by bread and wine, so are our souls by these tokens of the body and blood of Christ."[45] For Wesley, the physical act of taking Communion is inseparable from the spiritual benefits that it confers.

Of course, this interconnectedness can run the other way, too, from the spiritual to the physical. Wesley will affirm that many physical afflictions have spiritual causes. According to Wesley, the disordered passions that flow from our corrupted will can cause disease,[46] and he also believes that much sickness—especially mental illness—is directly caused by demonic forces.[47] This is why Wesley believes that "no man can be a thorough physician without being an experienced Christian."[48]

A positive flow from the spirit to the body is also possible, however. Wesley thinks that having a healthy spiritual life does as much as anything else to promote physical health as well. As he notes at the close of his introduction to *Primitive Physick*: "The love of God, as it is the sovereign remedy of all miseries, so in particular it effectually prevents all the bodily disorders the passions introduce, by keeping the passions themselves within due bounds. And by the unspeakable joy, and perfect calm, serenity, and tranquility it gives the mind, it becomes the most powerful of all the means of health and long life."[49]

If human beings *are* embodied spirits, and God is going to save them as such, then salvation will have both physical and spiritual effects. Some Christian traditions focus solely on the spiritual effects of God's work. This often implies a view of salvation as "going to heaven when you die," and it may make little difference in day-to-day life. Other Christian traditions focus so much on physical issues here and now—perhaps emphasizing things like social justice or how to live a happy life—that spiritual matters are of little importance. Wesley's view of human beings, by contrast, offers a balanced view that avoids these extremes. So, for example, proper diet and exercise go hand in hand with worship and spiritual devotions as part of living as embodied spirits. When someone is sick, one both prays for their healing and takes them to a doctor. Within human experience, the spiritual and the physical, the sacred and the secular, are distinct realities, but they are always found together. We always live with a foot in each of these worlds.

These, then, are the basic contours of Wesley's biblically grounded intuitions about what it means to be human—or at least what it meant to be so when God created humanity. Something, however, has gone wrong, and we do not find ourselves living today in the blissful situation that this picture of human nature paints. That "something" is sin. What that is and how that has compromised our God-given human nature is the subject of the next chapter.

eleven
Wesley's Thoughts on Sin

*T*he last piece we need on the table before we can engage Wesley's thoughts on salvation—the centerpiece of his theology—is the idea of sin. Given Wesley's high view of the goodness of God's original creation, we can see that sin was not part of God's original plan. If sin had not happened, there would be no need of salvation. However, it did happen, and the world we live in now is not the world as it was originally created to be. In many of Wesley's evangelistic sermons, he would start by outlining the problem he was addressing before moving on to offer God's solution to that problem, and so beginning the story of the drama of salvation with sin is simply following Wesley's own approach.

We will begin our examination of Wesley's thoughts on sin by looking at his understanding of the fall, which is where sin started, particularly "original sin," the way the effects of that fall are passed down to us today. We will then look at sin itself, highlighting its nature as a corruption of God's image in us. That corruption is displayed in our acts of rebellion, but it springs from a deeper source. With Wesley's understanding of our fallen condition, then, we will finally be prepared to hear the good news as Wesley wishes to proclaim it.

The Fall

Up to this point, we have allowed Wesley to paint a very positive picture of the relational goodness of the eternal God, of creation, and of human beings created in God's image. This picture, however, is at odds with our experience. Our world appears to be full of evil. Unless Wesley is describing some fantasy world far removed from our own, something must have happened to get the world that God made—a good world designed to get even better—so far off track. For Wesley, that was the fall.

In Wesley's reading of the Bible, the fall is unquestionably a historical event, and it is the event that explains why the world now is not the world as it ought to be. It explains why our experience is tainted and cannot wholly be trusted outside of the correction Scripture gives it. It explains why there is death and pain and distance from God, not just among humans, but in all of the created order. And it presents us with the fundamental obstacles that God's saving work must overcome in order to restore to human beings and the rest of God's creation their original goodness and to even take it further.

The dynamics of the fall appear to be pretty simple in Wesley's view, though no less tragic for all that. Adam and Eve were created completely good, with a "perfect" reflection of the image of God in all its facets—natural, political, and moral. At first, they lived out this image perfectly and so had a perfect set of relationships—with God, with each other, and with the rest of God's created order. However, part of their perfection was the gift of liberty or self-determination. This gift was designed to be exercised by the man and the woman in love, the original orientation out of which God created them and in which they were to live and be happy. Being created to love meant that they were supposed to orient themselves toward the outside: toward God, each other, and the creation that they were created to steward. Had they kept this orientation and exercised their freedom properly, everything would have functioned the way God had originally intended. But for freedom to be real, it had to be tested. "The liberty of man necessarily required that he should have some trial; else he would have had no choice whether he would stand or no, that is, no liberty at all. In order to this necessary trial, God said unto him, 'Of every tree in the garden thou mayest freely eat, but of the tree of the knowledge of good and evil, thou shalt not eat of it.'"[1]

So the full functioning of liberty demanded that a choice be set before Adam, and that choice was articulated by a law, a boundary line inscribing the relationship that he had with God. Thus God's love for Adam expressed itself in giving Adam the freedom to love God back. In the light of this boundary line, Adam could choose to keep the relationship intact or to break it. It is important to note that, for Wesley, it was the relationship, much more than the fruit, that was really at issue in this command.

Everyone knows what happened next. Inexplicably, Adam and Eve used their gift of freedom to turn away from God and to focus on themselves. This turning away from God broke their relationship with God, and that, in turn, led to them breaking God's law. The relational violation came first; for Wesley, the lawbreaking second.[2] This act was the event that moved creation away from the good state in which it was created to the evil-prone state that we experience. For Wesley, all pain, evil, sin, and death are rooted in this misuse of freedom. God gave human beings freedom so that they could be capable of love, and they were fully capable of exercising their freedom in perfectly loving ways.[3] But the gift of freedom also entailed the risk of evil. But that was a risk that God was apparently willing to take.

When Adam and Eve chose to be selfish rather than loving, they broke their relationships with God, each other, and the world in a way that they could not then repair. All the other consequences of their sin, both for them and their descendants, flowed from this break. Thus they lost both their good relationship with God ("God's favor," Wesley calls it) and the image of God that made that relationship possible.[4] However, before we look at the ways in which our present condition derives from these events, we have to say something about how Wesley understands the fall in the great scheme of redemption.

Wesley is sensitive to the charge that God is somehow at fault for the evil that resulted from the fall because God knew it was going to happen and God could have prevented it. Wesley acknowledges that these statements are true, but he claims that God chose to allow the fall because God planned to bring greater, eternal good out of these lesser and temporary evils. Because God permitted the fall, we have the demonstration of God's love for us in Christ that we would not have had otherwise. We also have God's promise that things will eventually be better than even God's originally created "perfection" (as we noted in the previous chapter). Wesley, then, seems to be a proponent of the idea of the fall often labeled *felix culpa* (Latin for "happy fault"). This tradition understands that the fall itself is not a good thing, but it is something that God makes into a good thing retroactively, as it were, because of the good that God eventually brings out of it.

Original Sin

Because of the fall, Wesley believes that we human beings today inherit the conditions of broken relationship that Adam and Eve created. Following his

Anglican tradition, he called this inherited condition of brokenness "original sin." Though he described the nature and effect of original sin differently at different times in his life, the *fact* of the matter was always important to him—so important that one could not have Christianity without it.

Traditional Christianity was under increasing attack in the intellectual climate of eighteenth-century England, even as ordinary people were responding in droves to Wesley's message. One major prong of that intellectual attack was an affirmation of human goodness and human capacity. Some intellectuals were beginning to claim that if society could educate people well enough, a good society would naturally emerge. Once people knew the good that they should do, they would naturally do it. In that case, human beings were masters of their own fate, and it did not make much sense to talk about the "need to be saved." There were even a few who saw the idea of a God who punishes people for doing evil and rewards them for doing good as a "primitive" form of morality that needed to fade for true human flourishing to emerge.

Wesley's reading of the Bible, however, gave him little reason to go along with that analysis. In fact, it encouraged the opposite belief. His most succinct portrayal of that reality was his sermon "Original Sin,"[5] framed as an explication of Gen. 6:5: "And God saw that the wickedness of man was great in the earth, and that every imagination of the thoughts of his heart was only evil continually" (KJV). Wesley interpreted this verse to mean two things. First, the fallen condition we inherit from our first parents affects everyone, no exceptions. There are no "good people," so there is no one who does not need the salvation that God provides in Christ.[6] Second, not only does original sin affect all people, but it also affects everything about them. No part of human life is free from this disease, since it goes all the way to the root of our actions and attitudes. In Wesley's words:

> Now God "saw that all" this, the whole thereof, "was evil," contrary to moral rectitude; contrary to the nature of God, which necessarily includes all good; contrary to the divine will, the eternal standard of good and evil; contrary to the pure, holy image of God, wherein man was originally created . . . contrary to justice, mercy, and truth, and to the essential relations which each man bore to his Creator and his fellow creatures.[7]

Since God is the only source of goodness, and since the human race had cut itself off from God, human beings cannot exhibit any goodness on their own. To believe otherwise was, in Wesley's mind, to deny the entire Christian religion. His logic was simple. If people are capable of saving themselves, then Christ's work on the cross was not necessary. However, if Christ's work on the cross was, indeed, necessary, then there is no way people could ever save themselves. The affirmation of Christ's work was linked to humanity's need for that work. The idea of original sin was, in a sense, the logical starting point for all of the ideas about Christian salvation that Wesley felt to be important. As he says later in the conclusion to that sermon: "From hence we may learn one grand, fundamental difference between Christianity, considered as a system of doctrines, and the most refined heathenism. . . . Is man by nature filled with all manner of evil? Is he void of all good? Is he wholly fallen? . . . Allow this, and you are so far a Christian. Deny it, and you are but an heathen still."[8]

So while Wesley believed that human beings were originally created to be good by God, their goodness no longer functions properly. Even though some of the image of God remains (in understanding or will or liberty), humans no longer use it to relate in love to God, others, and the rest of God's created order (those "essential relations," as he called them above). Human beings are now left in what Wesley misleadingly labels a "natural" state, by which he means human beings on their own—apart from God and spiritually dead.[9] The idea is an abstraction for Wesley, since he believed God left no one on his or her own, but it is an important abstraction nonetheless. Our spiritual deadness is where our experience "naturally" begins, and so it is where God begins the application of salvation to our individual lives.

During his Oxford years, Wesley articulated inherited deadness in strongly biological terms, even attempting to describe how the physical act of eating the forbidden fruit introduced physical conditions that could be passed down from Adam and Eve to their children.[10] During the early years of the revival, Wesley shifted his emphasis toward a more legal idea, treating Adam like a representative of humanity whose actions have consequences that his children inherit. In this typical Protestant view, human beings today are born "dead to God" as part of the punishment for Adam's sin. Eventually, however, Wesley decided that this view compromised God's justice, since it meant holding us accountable for something we did not do. This led him to return to a more biological-based idea of the transmission of original sin by the end of his life. However it comes to us, though, original sin means that we are now disposed to act in the same ways that Adam acted, incurring the same guilt and punishment he did. And so it is to the nature of present sin that we must now turn.

Sin and the Corruption of the Image of God

The fact that Wesley shifted his understanding of how original sin worked shows that ideas about sin were alive and active in his mind. Wesley was not content simply to affirm the truth of our inherent spiritual deadness; he analyzed it. Here, Wesley's ideas on sin align very well with his intuitions about human nature as articulated in his concept of the image of God, so we will use that concept as our guide. Wesley himself makes this connection by using the same words to describe sin that he uses to describe that image. His various concerns about sin make the most sense when seen in the light of his intuition that sin is essentially a corruption of the image of God in which human beings were created.

Sin and the Relational Image

As we noted in the previous chapter, the basic idea of the image of God for Wesley was that it made human beings "capable of God." They could relate to God in personal and loving ways better than anything else in the material creation. When Adam and Eve misused their freedom and turned away from God, they lost this relational capacity. Human beings became "incapable of God." They broke relationship by their disobedience, and—since their ability to relate to God was itself a product of God's relationship to them—they lost the capacity for relationship along with the relationship itself. It was as if they locked God out of their lives and threw away the key. The relationship was lost, along with any possibility of fixing it from their end.

In this sense, the full image of God in humanity was lost. Pieces of the image remain, as we will explore below, but they can no longer function as they once did to keep human beings in relationship with God. In fact, the fragments of God's image in us tend now to function only in ways that pull people farther and farther away from God and each other. And human beings in their "natural" state—on their own without God's help—are utterly incapable of fixing this problem.

Originally, God had articulated that boundary line that gave humanity freedom to love or reject God as a law. Therefore, the relational gap Adam and Eve created by violating that boundary can be thought of as legal guilt. This idea of sin forms the backbone of most theology about sin in the West, and Wesley shares this inheritance—though he prefers to use legal concepts to point to something deeper, such as the "law of love." In a legal context, the idea of guilt does not refer to the feelings associated with wrongdoing but rather to the objective fact of wrongness. When we violate a relational boundary or break a law, we *are* guilty regardless of how we feel about it. Until that objective guilt is dealt with, we can no longer relate to the person we have wronged or relate well in the society whose laws we have broken.

The normal way, of course, that guilt is dealt with is punishment. Once an offender pays the fine or serves time in prison, the "debt to society" is paid, the "guilt" is atoned for, and relationships can resume. But if the punishment for the offense is death—as it was clearly articulated to Adam and Eve—then the offender could not simply take the punishment and move on. Both the guilt and its punishment take away the possibility of a relationship with the one offended. So in the case of God and human beings, human beings are stuck. This idea is important for Wesley, since it grounds the entire story of salvation in grace. God does something for us that we could never do for ourselves.

Guilt, of course, does not magically appear in a person. It is produced by actions, actions that we normally call sins. To understand those actions, however, we must move beyond the general loss of the image of God in humanity to the specific ways in which humanity's natural image of God (the capacity for understanding, will, and liberty) and the moral image (the orientation toward goodness) have been corrupted in anti-relational ways.

Sin and the Natural and Moral Image

One of Wesley's most well-known ideas is his definition of sin as "a voluntary [or willful] transgression of a known law of God."[11] Though not unique to Wesley, the phrase ties his understanding of sin to his concept of the image of God. Wesley articulated the natural image of God as understanding, will, and liberty. Sin, then, is an exercise of liberty—a choice—that involves both the will (with all of its desires, tempers, and affections) and the understanding. Such acts result from a deep corruption of our nature. Therefore, just as guilt is the result of acts of sin, so acts of sin are the result of something deeper.

Actual sin. Wesley insists that the only actions that qualify as sins are those relationally disruptive actions that involve liberty, will, and understanding. "Nothing is sin, strictly speaking," he writes, "but a voluntary transgression of a known law of God. Therefore every voluntary breach of the law of love is sin; and nothing else, if we speak properly."[12] This is a true definition for Wesley, not merely a description. All voluntary transgressions are sin, and only voluntary transgressions are sin. This makes his concept of sin broad enough to include anything that knowingly violates relationships (the "law of love," as Wesley puts it), even if the Bible doesn't say anything about it. But it also narrows the definition to only those actions that arise from our corrupted nature. Only those actions that are rebellious qualify as sins. The reason for this insistence is twofold.

First of all, Wesley understands that God's laws can be broken in ways that do not involve the understanding or the will. People make mistakes in their ignorance and cause unintended or accidental disruptions in their relationships. Such mistakes still require forgiveness, and when they are committed against God, they need to be covered by the atoning sacrifice of Christ. However, Wesley insists that these involuntary or unknowing actions cannot properly be labeled as sins. They arise from our limited physical nature, so we must deal with them, but they do not make us "guilty."

If we treat these violations as though they were sins, according to Wesley, we make the problem of sin unsolvable. Wesley accuses the Calvinists of this mistake,[13] and it saps any motivation we might have for dealing seriously with sin. After all, if we mess up our relationships because we are finite and mortal, and we cannot do anything about that, why bother trying? It is true that we need the constant forgiveness of God and others for the accidental ways we compromise our relationships. However, acts that are deliberately and knowingly disruptive indicate a deeper problem than simple finitude. After all, there is a difference between accidentally stepping on someone's toe and deliberately grinding a heel into his or her foot. This brings us to the second reason why Wesley wants to reserve the label "sin" for willful and knowing acts.

Wesley is not simply interested in the fact of our breaking God's laws; he wants to know the source of those actions. What kind of person deliberately and knowingly grinds his heel into another person's foot? What kind of people knowingly and willfully reject God's boundary lines and try to set themselves up as gods in God's place? That seems like a crazy thing to do, but human beings do it anyway. Why? What's wrong with them? Wesley's definition of sin thus points to deeper problems in our nature than simply inadequate performance. By defining sin as rebellion, Wesley highlights the corruption in our understanding and will that leads to our relationally disruptive behavior in the first place. It also indicates that our whole sense of good (the moral image) must be messed up as well. Wesley's definition of the act of sin shows us that sin is more than just an act. Something is driving it. Sin is not just outward acts but an inward disposition as well.

Inbred sin. Wesley has a number of names for the source of our sinful actions, but all of them refer to something that is inward—as opposed to the outward manifestations of sin that are our transgressions. He sometimes calls it "indwelling sin,"[14] sometimes "inbred sin,"[15] and sometimes a "principle."[16] Whatever Wesley calls it, however, the intent is the same. Somewhere lodged in the inner core of our personhood is an orientation out of which all of our outward actions flow. That principle or fount was originally created to be and act like God, but it has been completely corrupted. It is now, to use Wesley's favorite verses on the subject, an "evil tree" that can only grow "evil fruit" (see Matt. 7:18; Luke 6:43).

This corruption is a corruption of both the natural and moral image of God in humanity. To begin with, it is a corruption of our understanding. In one sense, it is a lack of understanding. Wesley will frequently use the metaphor of blindness to highlight this part of our debilitated human condition. We are blind to the truth, blind to our own nature, and blind to anything good that could move us toward God. Because we have no understanding of God, our will cannot desire or want God, and so we cannot love God or relate to God.[17] The problem, however, is deeper than ignorance. We do not just lack knowledge; we think we know things that we actually do not know. Our understanding leads us to think of things as good that are actually evil.[18] Our understanding, thus, leads us to act in ways entirely opposite to what it was created to do.

Just as our understanding has turned to folly, our will has turned to selfishness. As we saw in the last chapter, the human will was created to want the good, to love and desire what God wanted. The fallen will, however, now only wants its own desires and refuses to reorient them toward God's. Our affections "naturally" (i.e., godlessly) tend toward the things of this material world now rather than the things of God. Even our willful habits of desire—our "tempers" Wesley calls them—have been trained toward things that increase our unhappiness rather than our happiness, our destruction rather than our salvation.[19] In Wesley's eyes, human beings apart from God are so far gone that they do not even want to be saved. Finally, in the face of a corrupt understanding and a selfish will, whatever liberty remained to human beings is powerless to choose God and becomes enslaved to ignorance, folly, and sin.

The corruption of our understanding and will and the loss of liberty thus go hand in hand with the loss of our moral image of God. Human beings no longer have an orientation toward the good or toward God. Even though God created them for holiness and righteousness, they now only pursue sin. Even though God created them to love God and others, they only pursue their own selfish desires. What they understand and will as "good" is actually evil, and they don't know it, and they don't care. Humanity, then, is truly and utterly lost.

If human beings have been this deeply corrupted, then we need more than just forgiveness for the bad things we have done. We are guilty, to be sure, but there is a deeper sickness that is feeding that guilt. Something must be radically wrong with us if we want to do the things that make us guilty. But as deep as Wesley understands the problem of sin to be—and it's hard to see how it could be any deeper—Wesley sees God's solution to the problem of sin as deeper still. In those places where Wesley emphasizes the depths of the fall, he makes sure to emphasize the even greater depths of grace.[20] It is to such grace that we can now proceed.

twelve
Wesley's Thoughts on Salvation (1)

We finally come to Wesley's thoughts on salvation, which, as we have said, is the centerpiece of his theology. As Wesley said in the preface to his first volume of sermons, "I want to know one thing, the way to heaven."[1] For Wesley, "the way to heaven" was found in the renewal of the image of God, which he variously labeled the pursuit of holiness, sanctification, or Christian perfection. The God who is love created a world that could serve as an environment for loving relationships and a people in God's image who were capable of them. Though they have lost this capacity through sin, God still wants that relationship. And so God's work of salvation is a work of new creation, restoring what was lost so that love can flourish as it was originally designed to do.

Seen in this light, Wesley's understanding of salvation is a distinctive one, a thoughtful combination of various Christian traditions stamped with his own emphases and insights. In spite of that, however, little of what we discuss in this chapter should come as any surprise. If we understand Wesley's fundamental intuitions and confessions about God, about creation and human beings, and about the problem of sin, then we will find his understanding of salvation to be relatively easy to predict. Once we see the dots, they almost connect themselves. In this chapter, we will look at the basic pieces Wesley puts together to form his doctrine of salvation. In the next chapter, we will look in detail at the way those pieces work their way out in the drama of salvation.

We will approach Wesley's thoughts on salvation in a way similar to the way we approached his thoughts on sin—with the historical events that set the stage for everything that follows. For Wesley, these are the life, death, and resurrection of Jesus Christ and the coming of the Holy Spirit on Pentecost. From there, we will look at Wesley's basic understanding of grace and faith, the two sets of responses, one might say—one from God's side and one from ours—that shape everything that happens in the process of salvation. The final section of this chapter will be an overview of the "order of salvation" (or *ordo salutis*, in Latin), which will form the framework for our more detailed look at the process of salvation in the following chapter.

Salvation: The Historical Anchors

As we saw in the last chapter, Wesley viewed the fall as a historical act with historical consequences. In the same way, Wesley understood that God's saving acts were also historical acts, and they, too, have ongoing, real-world consequences. The saving acts of God through Christ and the Holy Spirit actually began the moment Adam and Eve sinned, and they continued throughout history.[2] They were, however, given new prominence and a new level of effectiveness when Christ was born into the world and the Holy Spirit was given to Christ's followers at Pentecost.

Christ

Wesley does not have a highly developed or nuanced reflection on the person and work of Christ. If anything, his reflections on Christ may be the weakest part of his theological system. Most of Wesley's interpreters have recognized that he simply assumes a basic Protestant understanding about Christ and moves on from there to talk about the role of Christ in salvation. He preaches only one sermon on an explicit aspect of Christ's identity, and in that sermon he emphasizes Christ's divinity so strongly that Christ's humanity seems overshadowed.[3] Nevertheless, while this is a problem, it still serves to underscore the historical and God-initiated character of the events that secure our salvation.

Wesley's strong emphasis on Christ's divinity highlights the fact that it is God and God alone who initiates and accomplishes human salvation. It is God who conceives the plan of saving humanity through the death of Christ on the cross, and it is Christ as God who acquiesces to the plan and whose obedience allows it to succeed. In that way, salvation as new creation is like the first creation. Both are acts that only God can accomplish, and God performs them with no preconditions and simply out of God's own loving decision. Christ's divinity also underscores the importance of his teaching—since this would be seen as teaching that comes straight from the mouth of God—and Wesley preaches a thirteen-sermon series on the Sermon on the Mount that he publishes in his very first edition of sermons.[4]

Although Wesley focuses mostly on Christ's divinity, his humanity also plays a role in salvation. Christ is the only perfect expression of the image of God in a human life, and so he exemplifies our true human nature in a way that no one else has or could. His perfect human nature was expressed in perfect obedience to God, and his submission to God's will gives God a reason to extend God's favor to humanity again.[5] Recall that human beings lost both the favor (the good relationship) and the image of God in the fall. Christ, thus, empowers the process of undoing that fall in two ways. First, he becomes the vehicle through which God extends a relationship to humanity again. Second, he is the example of what the image of God lived out in relationship to God looks like.

The "new creation" work of God in Christ, like the work of the first creation, is something that God does in order to get a response from those creatures God created. And so, even though Christ accomplishes the fact of salvation, this fact still needs to be applied to individual lives and to communities. That application is brought about by the work of the third person of the Trinity, the Holy Spirit.

Holy Spirit

Since the events of the crucifixion and resurrection happened a long time ago, Wesley recognized that there needed to be some way for the saving work of Christ to be connected to the lives of those who were not around when those events happened. There needed to be some way to apply the historical work of Christ to other epochs of history. This is accomplished, for Wesley, by the work of the Holy Spirit, whose coming is also anchored in history by the events of Pentecost.

Wesley does not emphasize the event of Pentecost nearly as often as he emphasizes the events of Christ's passion, but its importance as a historical event in his thought is nevertheless clear. The events of the death and resurrection of Christ would be remote and ineffective had they not been applied to the lives of believers by the coming of the Holy Spirit. Wesley equates being Christian with being filled with the Holy Spirit,[6] and he is explicit about the fact that the full range of God's saving grace was only available after Christ had ascended into heaven and sent the Holy Spirit to apply his work.[7] And so, it is about the day of Pentecost and the birth of the church—and not about the day of Christ's resurrection—that Wesley rhapsodizes in saying:

Here was the dawn of the proper gospel day. Here was a proper Christian church. It was now "the Sun of righteousness rose" upon the earth, "with healing in his wings." He did now "save his people from their sins": he "healed" all "their sickness." He not only taught that religion which is true "healing of the soul," but effectually planted it in the earth; filling the souls of all that believed in him with *righteousness*, gratitude to God, and good-will to man, attended with a *peace* that surpassed all understanding, and with *joy* unspeakable and full of glory.[8]

To be sure, for Wesley, the Holy Spirit is the Spirit of Christ,[9] and this affir-mation, too, stems from his emphasis on the divinity of Christ and of the Holy Spirit, since their divine nature is what unites them. Still, the work of Christ in his death and resurrection and the work of the Holy Spirit in Pentecost are not the same, and the difference is important. One way to look at the difference is this. Christ comes to establish the potential for salvation; the Holy Spirit makes that potential real. It is the Holy Spirit that empowers believers to live out their life of salvation, sanctifies them, renews the image of God in them, and assures them of their newly restored favor with God.[10] The application of salvation, however, is not done merely by imposition or imputation. It happens when God acts and human beings respond. The terms of this action and response are found in Wesley's understanding of grace and faith.

Grace and Faith

The terms "grace" and "faith" are common theological terms, but that does not mean their meanings are always evident. Wesley uses these terms to refer to God's action and our response in the application of Christ's saving work to our lives today. Taken together, they illustrate the fundamental dynamic that drives the process of salvation for Wesley.

Grace

As we saw when we surveyed his thoughts on God, Wesley has some clas-sical intuitions about God's complete otherness and independence from the world. When it comes to God's saving work, this means all of God's actions are uncompelled and free. God doesn't *have* to do anything when it comes to salvation; if God does anything at all, it arises out of God's free choice. These intuitions also mean that any interaction between God and the world happens ultimately on God's initiative. So God always makes the first move, and these moves are all the result of God's loving choices and nothing else. Wesley's label for these loving first moves of God is "grace."

Over and over again, Wesley stresses that God's grace is free. Humanity is completely fallen and distant from God, and so there is nothing any human could do to earn God's favor or compel God's activity. God's work needs no preconditions and isn't a response to something human beings have already done. Since Wesley has often been accused of preaching a works-righteousness, his emphasis on this point is worth quoting in some detail.

The grace or love of God, whence cometh our salvation, is free in all, and free for all.

First, it is free in all to whom it is given. It does not depend on any power or merit in man; no, not in any degree, neither in whole, nor in part. It does not in any wise depend either on the good works or righteousness of the receiver; not on anything he has done, or anything he is. It does not depend on his endeavours. It does not depend on his good tempers, or good desires, or good purposes and intentions; for all these flow from the free grace of God. They are the streams only, not the fountain. They are the fruits of free grace, and not the root. They are not the cause, but the effects of it. Whatsoever good is in man, or is done by man, God is the author and doer of it. Thus is his grace free in all, that is, no way depending on any power or merit in man, but on God alone, who freely gave us his own Son, and "with him freely giveth us all things."[11]

Wesley is clear—God is the sole Initiator of the process of salvation, and that salvation is by grace alone. However, this passage also indicates that the effect of grace, perhaps even the very purpose of it, is to empower human response. In other words, Wesley understands the work of grace not just to be something God does *for* human beings—though it certainly is that. He specifically says that it is something God does *in* human beings, something God does so that human beings can do something in return.

The other affirmation that Wesley finds so important to make about grace is that it is "free for all," meaning that God extends God's loving activity to every member of the human race. Unlike those who preached salvation as something only for a select few whom God had chosen, Wesley claimed that the saving grace of God excluded no one. This further emphasizes grace's empowering character, since not everyone to whom grace is extended ends up getting saved. The Calvinists saw grace as an irresistible or overpowering work of God, which means it always accomplished its goal. For them, the logic was clear. If there is grace, then there is salvation. This also meant that if there is no salvation, then there is no grace. This lack of grace among those who are not saved is explained by the fact that they were not chosen by God for salvation and thus were left to their own devices. And the inevitable result of that was hell.

Wesley found such a conclusion abhorrent and so emphasized an idea of grace as an empowering or enabling work. Grace is what restores the possibility of turning to God and relating to God, which humanity had lost through sin and the fall. But that meant that there could be some—wholly against God's express will and desire (2 Pet. 3:9)—who reject God's offer of grace. "'The power of the Lord is present to heal them,'" Wesley writes, "but they will not be healed. They 'reject the counsel,' the merciful counsel 'of God against themselves,' as did their stiff-necked forefathers. And therefore are they without excuse, because God would save them, but they will not be saved."[12]

God's salvation is all about restoring the image of God in human beings, and part of that image is the idea of liberty or freedom. Grace, then, in part restores this liberty so that people are free again to choose God. But that liberty can also be used—as Adam himself originally used it—to choose evil. Such a choice is essentially a rejection of God's creative and re-creative grace.

Faith

So, grace is the active love of God extended to human beings in a way designed to empower them to love God back. While this grace empowers lots of different kinds of responses, as Wesley noted in the long quote above, the fundamental response, the one that grounds all of the others, is what Wesley calls faith.

Early in his life, Wesley held a rather traditional view of faith as merely the assent to the truth of some proposition. Faith was the affirmation that you believed *that* something was true. His mother, Susanna, however, helped him to see past this merely intellectual idea of faith to something more relational, something that included trust. As he notes in his sermon "Salvation by Faith," "It [faith] is not barely a speculative, rational thing, a cold, lifeless assent, a train of ideas in the head; but also a disposition of the heart."[13] This is not to say that faith has no intellectual side in Wesley, merely that full Christian faith also needs to be something more. Merely rational faith with no relational component is something Wesley provocatively calls the "faith of a devil."[14]

The intellectual component of faith for Wesley was anchored in his understanding of Hebrews 11:1. In that verse, he would highlight the idea of faith as a "conviction" or "assurance," even using the original Greek word for "conviction" in his sermons.[15] Faith was what allowed us to *know* the spiritual world in a way that was analogous to the way our physical senses allow us to know the physical world. This idea of faith as a "spiritual sense," a means by which we acquire knowledge, was an important—if somewhat controversial—idea of Wesley.[16] Scholars debate about just how rigorous a philosophical idea it was, but the orientation of the idea is clear. If there is a spiritual world, our fallen physical senses have no access to it, as we have already explored. God, however, gives us this access, because without the knowledge of God and of this spiritual world, it would be impossible for us to relate to God.

This brings us to the second and more important part of faith. Faith as knowledge is designed to serve faith as trust. Wesley's favorite way to talk about this part of faith was to use the definition provided by his Anglican tradition, a definition that he uses throughout his sermons and letters whenever he wants to emphasize the relational side of faith.

> "The right and true Christian faith is" (to go on in the words of our own Church) "not only to believe that Holy Scripture and the articles of our faith are true, but also to have a sure trust and confidence to be saved from everlasting damnation by Christ"—it is a "sure trust and confidence" which a man hath in God "that by the merits of Christ his sins *are* forgiven, and he reconciled to the favour of God"—"whereof doth follow a loving heart to obey his commandments."[17]

To Wesley, it is this kind of faith that makes one "not *almost* only, but *altogether* a Christian."[18]

Faith, then, includes both an intellectual quality of understanding and an affective quality of the will, and so it represents the renewal of two facets of God's image in us. Once we recognize that real faith is always faith "working in love" (see Gal. 5:6), the third facet—liberty—shows up as well. Faith gives us understanding of the world from God's perspective, aligns our will to God's will through trust and obedience, and directs our liberty toward loving choices. Furthermore, Wesley was explicit that this faith could only come as a result of grace. It was the "gift of God," not something anyone could muster up on his or her own.[19]

These, then, are the twin dynamics that drive Wesley's soteriology (theology of salvation). On the side of God, there is grace, the empowering work of God that enables human beings who are dead in their sins to turn to God and live again. The acceptance of this grace is an act of faith, a knowing and "sure trust and confidence." We will now turn to a brief overview of the specific ways in which God's grace works to empower the response of faith so that human beings can live in loving relationship with God, with one another, and with the rest of God's created order.

The *Ordo Salutis*

As part of his inheritance from the Protestant tradition, Wesley tended to see God's salvation as following a basic pattern. That pattern is usually labeled in Latin as the *ordo salutis*, the "order of salvation." Wesley lays out this basic pattern in several places (one of which we'll explore below), and he paints a consistent picture each time. As God is at work and people respond, certain things tend to happen in a certain order. Sometimes God is doing multiple things at the same time, but teasing them apart still helps us get a better sense of the larger reality of salvation. For Wesley, that means the restoration and renewal of the image of God in human beings.

However, while Wesley has an understanding of the typical pattern of God's work, he also recognizes that talking about these patterns is for our benefit. They do not bind God in any way. God remains independent and has complete freedom to act as God chooses. "The dealings of God with man are infinitely varied," Wesley writes to one of his correspondents, "and cannot be confined to any general rule; both in justification and sanctification He often acts in a manner we cannot account for."[20]

Thus the *ordo salutis* in Wesley is not a straightjacket on God or an infallible road map. Rather, it is a set of expectations we can use as we cooperate with God now and hope for what God yet wants to do in the future. We must, however, hold these expectations loosely, trusting that God's ways are best. As Wesley notes to another of his correspondents, "Sometimes it pleases our Lord to work a great deliverance even of this kind in a moment. Sometimes He gives the victory by degrees. And I believe this is more common. Expect this and every good gift from Him. How wise and gracious are all His ways!"[21]

Wesley gives us a brief overview of how he sees the process of salvation, the *ordo salutis*, in his sermon "On Working Out Our Own Salvation." We will let this establish our general framework before we explore it in greater depth in the next chapter. Wesley writes,

> Salvation begins with what is usually termed (and very properly) "preventing [prevenient] grace"; including the first wish to please God, the first dawn of light concerning his will, and the first slight, transient conviction of having sinned against him. All these imply some tendency toward life, some degree of salvation, the beginning of a deliverance from a blind, unfeeling heart, quite insensible of God and the things of God. Salvation is carried on by "convincing grace," usually in Scripture termed "repentance," which brings a larger measure of self-knowledge, and a farther deliverance from the heart of stone. Afterwards we experience the proper Christian salvation, whereby "through grace" we "are saved by faith," consisting of those two grand branches, justification and sanctification. By justification we are saved from the guilt of sin, and restored to the favour of God: by sanctification we are saved from the power and root of sin, and restored to the image of God. All experience, as well as Scripture, shows this salvation to be both instantaneous and gradual. It begins the moment we are justified, in the holy, humble, gentle, patient love of God and man. It gradually increases from that moment, as a "grain of mustard seed, which at first is the least of all seeds, but" gradually "puts forth large branches," and becomes a great tree; till in another instant the heart is cleansed from all sin, and filled with pure love to God and man. But even that love increases more and more, till we "grow up in all things into him that is our head," "till we attain the measure of the stature of the fullness of Christ."[22]

God's saving work is God's response to humanity's rejection of God's original offer of relationship in creation. Because of the fall and original sin, it was easy—even inevitable—for every human being after Adam to follow in Adam's footsteps. All humanity has turned away from God and lost both the fact of a relationship with God and even the very ability to relate to God. God must then start with a broken creature that has no true understanding, a self-focused will, and no real ability to choose the good any longer. Furthermore, this creature has lost its orientation toward true goodness—God's goodness—and so has a confused moral compass. So, the natural image of God (understanding, will, and liberty) and the moral image of God (orientation toward goodness) have been lost, and without these, humanity cannot relate to God. And so this is where God begins to restore that relationship.

Since fallen human beings have no awareness of the spiritual world, God must first act independently of them and without their knowledge. This is the grace that must "come before" any possibility of response (because those responses are only made possible by this grace), and so we call it "prevenient grace." Like the image of God, the work of prevenient grace is threefold. Its first job is to awaken the understanding so that human beings become aware of God and what God wants for them. This also comes with an awareness of their fallen and broken condition and how far they are from what God wants them to be. This awakening work usually goes by the label "conviction" in Wesley, and its chief instrument is the law. The law is a clear articulation of the boundary line around humanity's relationship with God, and it shows exactly how human beings have transgressed that relationship. If human beings accept this new knowledge of God, of themselves, and of what is needed for a relationship with God, then it will empower the will. Freed from its self-focus, the will can now desire something outside of itself—namely God and what God wants. This renewed understanding and renewed desire set up an act of liberty that allows a proper relationship with God to begin.

The choice to turn away from one's former life toward a new life with God is an act of faith known as repentance. At first—given the role of law in conviction—this new life with God is usually oriented by a desire to know and do the will of God in obedience. Wesley calls this level of faith the "faith of a servant."[23] This is a proper step toward God and God accepts it, but such an "external" orientation is not the ultimate goal. Wesley is most concerned about relationships, and so he understands that the more mature step of faith is the one where we come into a truly personal relationship with God, which Wesley calls the "faith of a son."[24] This, properly speaking for Wesley, is the moment of full conversion, the saving moment. Through the power of the Holy Spirit on the basis of the atonement of Christ, we are returned to the favor of God in justification, and we begin a new life with God in regeneration, new birth, and initial sanctification.

In many Protestant traditions, even evangelical ones, this is the climax of the story of salvation, the moment when the sinner is turned back to God and given the promise of new life and heaven. For Wesley, however, this is just the introduction. The best parts are yet to come. Converted sinners are only just beginning to relate well to God and others, only just beginning to live out the law of love and the image of God that they were created to express. The understanding is not fully "healed," and there are actions and attitudes that hamper relationships in their own lives of which they are still unaware. Their will has been freed from its bondage to the self, but they still find selfish desires rising up and inducing them to act in very unloving ways. And although the guilt of sin has been removed, there are still many places where they know that their humanity falls short of the pattern given by Christ, places where they need more love, more joy, more peace, more patience, more of all the gifts that are the evidence of the Holy Spirit's work in a human life. The process of dying out to the self and becoming more like God is one that Wesley calls sanctification. This is where the complete renovation and renewal of the image of God takes place. Wesley has the audacity to believe that God can actually accomplish such a work in a human life, that God's sanctifying grace can lead a human being to a life filled with nothing but love, a life of entire sanctification. That is the ultimate goal of the grace of God at work in a human being.

This is but a brief summary of Wesley's understanding of the way salvation tends to happen most of the time, but all of the essential pieces are there. It now falls to us to explore this *ordo salutis* more fully, a task we will take up in the next chapter.

thirteen
Wesley's Thoughts on Salvation (2)

*N*ow that we have seen an overview of Wesley's thoughts on salvation in general, we can take a deeper look at the various pieces of that process. Seeing the pattern as Wesley sees it is helpful, at least as long as we avoid making this pattern a kind of law, as though every piece were always necessary or that this was the way it is "supposed to happen" for everyone. Wesley himself always wants to recognize God's freedom to act as God deems best. So we study this pattern in order to better cooperate with God, not to tell God what God is supposed to do.

We will start with the "preconversion" elements of Wesley's *ordo salutis*. These are the things God does to get our attention and help us turn away from ourselves and toward God again. This work we will group under the heading "Prevenient Grace."

In the second section, titled "Saving Grace," we will look at the relationship with God we call salvation. This includes, first, the idea of "full conversion," the maturing of faith from an external or objective orientation to an internal and relational reality. Wesley calls this having the "faith of a son," as opposed to merely having the "faith of a servant." Second, there is the act by which God restores us to God's favor by forgiving us of those violations of God's relational boundaries we call sins. "Justification" is the normal legal term that Wesley uses here. Third, there is God's reequipping of us so that we can more deeply pursue our relationship with God and more fully cooperate with God's restoration of the moral image of God in which we were created. "New birth," "regeneration," and "initial sanctification" are all phrases Wesley uses to refer to this process.

In the last section, titled "Sanctifying Grace," we will look at the goal of this saving work for individuals, which Wesley normally calls Christian perfection, but which can also be labeled entire sanctification. This is the state of perfect love in which God desires every human being to live. In exploring this, we will see Wesley's gift for balancing concerns that are so often in tension in the Christian life. All of salvation—sanctification is no exception—is a work of God. It is not something human beings do for themselves, and so it all depends on grace. The function of this grace, however, is to empower human activity, not replace it. In the working of this grace, Wesley displays both a profound optimism about what God can do along with a realistic view of the obstacles we humans face in cooperating with God's work. Finally, Wesley understands the work of God to contain both elements of process, that is, things that take time, and elements that are instantaneous, that is, things that happen in a moment. All of this gives us a balanced view of salvation and enables us to cooperate better with God and to encourage others in their cooperation with God.

Prevenient Grace: The Invitation to Renewal

Because of the fall, the "natural" state of human beings—human beings considered apart from any work of God—is one of incapacity. We are guilty, meaning out of favor with God, and we are spiritually dead, insensitive to God's realm. On our own, we only know and care about this physical world, and we tend to act in ways that enforce our spiritual—and hasten our physical—death. Because God's natural and moral image in us is lost or ineffective, we human beings have no moral compass. We have no understanding of God, no will or desire for God, therefore no liberty to choose the good things of God.

Prevenient Grace as Initial Favor

Wesley's diagnosis of our fallen condition matches that given by John Calvin and the other Protestant Reformers. In answering the question, "Does not the truth of the gospel lie very near both to Calvinism and Antinomianism?" Wesley famously replied, "Indeed it does—as it were, within a hair's breadth."[1] What distinguishes Wesley's view of salvation is what God does with that state of brokenness. Wesley's concept of prevenient grace forms the first crucial step down a path very different from the one taken by Calvin.

For the Reformers, God begins the process of salvation with two moves. First, God decides that some of those spiritually dead will be given spiritual life; these are the elect that God predestines to salvation. Second, God then applies an irresistible, power-like grace to their lives so that their guilt—but only theirs—is atoned for in Christ and their hearts are convicted of their sin, which makes them inevitably turn to God. So God demonstrates mercy to the elect, but to everyone else God demonstrates justice. God will give to the rest of humanity a "common grace" that keeps in check much of the natural tendency of humanity's depravity, but this is not a saving grace, and it makes no difference to anyone's eternal destiny.[2]

In sharp contrast to this, Wesley holds to the idea of "preventing" or "prevenient" grace.[3] Like the Reformed tradition of common grace, this is an undeserved favor of God that God extends to the entire human race. However, unlike common grace, Wesley's prevenient grace is designed to lead to "saving grace." It is grace given to start the process of restoring humanity's relationship with God and to restore enough of the image of God to make that possible. As we noted in the last chapter, Wesley thinks that God wants to save everyone. Since no one is capable of any move toward God without God's help, God would have to extend grace to everyone if God truly wanted everyone to be saved. Wesley thinks God did just that.

Since human beings in their natural state "ought" to be seen as guilty before God, the first part of prevenient grace is the recognition that God wants to restore all humanity to God's favor. Thus prevenient grace cancels any guilt associated with original sin. Even though Adam was humanity's legal representative and even though his guilt should be passed down to his children, God decides not to "press charges." No one today is condemned for Adam's sin back then. In response to the question, "In what sense is the righteousness of Christ imputed to all mankind, or to believers?" Wesley answers by quoting Romans 5:19 and affirming, "By the merits of Christ, all men are cleared from the guilt of Adam's actual sin."[4] If we are condemned, it is only because we, too, have sinned as Adam did—which, of course, Wesley believes we have.

To Wesley, Christ's very coming was a sign of God's favor to all humanity, but this is not enough to save it. Wesley understands salvation to be about relationship, and relationships are two-sided. Therefore, an independent act of God cannot create a mutual relationship between God and humanity. However, fallen human beings apart from God are no more capable of relating to God than rocks or trees. So the second part of God's prevenient grace restores some capacity for relating to God—God's image, in Wesley's terms. That image is threefold (understanding, will, and liberty), and so God's prevenient grace is threefold as well.

Prevenient Grace as Initial Renewal

Understanding. As a first sign of God's favor and the first move toward empowering us to relate to God again, prevenient grace begins to renew our understanding. Fallen human beings cannot know God, and they are blind to their own fallen condition. Wesley provides an extensive and eloquent description of this state in the first part of his sermon "Awake, Thou That Sleepest," where he describes the sinner in the following terms:

> Full of all diseases as he is, he fancies himself in perfect health. Fast bound in misery and iron, he dreams that he is happy and at liberty. . . . A fire is kindled around him, yet he knoweth it not; yea, it burns him, yet he lays it not to heart.
>
> . . . a sinner satisfied in his sins, contented to remain in his fallen state, to live and die without the image of God; one who is ignorant both of his disease and of the only remedy for it.[5]

So prevenient grace comes to awaken us and create awareness in us of God and of our own horrible condition. Without this awareness, we could never turn to God. Wesley calls this awakening work of prevenient grace "conviction" or "repentance," a confrontation with the truth about ourselves—along with its dire consequences—that only the work of the Holy Spirit can bring about.

Will. Knowing the truth, however, is not enough because our will has been corrupted as well. We no longer desire the truth or want to act on it. God's prevenient grace must stir up in us a desire for God, a desire that does not exist naturally in our fallen minds. If God did not do this, we could see the truth and still turn away from it. Wesley connects this stirring of our will with our conscience. The fact that we all have a conscience is, to Wesley, a demonstration of the nature and scope of prevenient grace.

> For allowing that all the souls of men are dead in sin by *nature*, this excuses none, seeing there is no man that is in a state of mere nature; there is no man, unless he has quenched the Spirit, that is wholly void of the grace of God. No man living is entirely destitute of what is vulgarly called "natural conscience." But this is not natural; it is more properly termed "preventing grace." . . . So that no man sins because he has not grace, but because he does not use the grace which he hath.[6]

Liberty. What Wesley means by "use the grace" is "respond to it." With an awakened understanding and a renewed will, we then have a new moment of liberty. We now have the opportunity to choose for God. A relationship with God must be chosen freely if it is to be a relationship at all, but that also means that God might work to create awareness and desire only to have that work rejected. Because the freedom restored to us at this point is a true freedom, people can close their eyes to their new knowledge and turn away from the new desires God has given them.

This moment of choice is the ultimate goal of prevenient grace, and it highlights the empowering or enabling nature of grace that we discussed in the last chapter. God could simply exercise God's power to accomplish God's purposes. But Wesley understands grace to be an exercise of God's love before it is an exercise of God's power. God acts to get a personal response, not to accomplish an impersonal task. God restores God's natural image in us so that we can "re-act" to God's work. This "re-action" is the whole point, and God takes our rejection of God's invitation very seriously. In Wesley's words,

> God does not continue to act upon the soul unless the soul re-acts upon God. He prevents [goes before] us indeed with the blessings of his goodness. He first loves us, and manifests himself unto us. While we are yet afar off he calls us to himself, and shines upon our hearts. But if we do not then love him who first loved us . . . his Spirit will not always strive; he will gradually withdraw, and leave us to the darkness of our own hearts.[7]

God's grace is a grace of love, not a grace of power. Wesley does not set God's work and our response at odds with one another, as if salvation were a task either that God accomplished or that we did for ourselves. God works so that we might work, not so that our work becomes unnecessary. "His influences," Wesley writes, "are not to supersede, but to encourage, our own efforts."[8] God's work is always first, and people cannot save themselves. But the very purpose of that work is to enable our own. It is, in Randy Maddox's well-known phrase, a "responsible grace."[9]

If we reject God's offer of relationship, God may graciously give us many other chances, but the freedom restored to us in that moment of grace is not something permanent. It is only a temporary freedom. Like the freedom to run a long-distance race or to play a complex piano piece, it is a freedom that must be properly used to be maintained. If we choose ourselves when we could choose for God, we may find ourselves again at the mercy of our own debilitated capacities. If, however, we cooperate with God and accept God's invitation of relationship, we move on into the next stages of our relationship with God. The act of turning away from ourselves and toward God is known as conversion, and that brings us from the work of prevenient grace to the work of saving grace.

Saving Grace: Conversion, Justification, and New Birth

Many of Wesley's evangelical descendants are used to thinking about salvation or conversion in dramatic and emotional terms. Wesley recognized the role of such conversions, but he also recognized a place for *partial* conversion. Wesley knew people who were partially turned toward God but lacked a true relationship with God. Wesley called this the state of an "Almost Christian," one who had the "faith of a servant" but lacked the "faith of a son." We will start our look at Wesley's thoughts on saving grace with that idea before turning to the intertwining realities of justification and new birth and the way they point us toward even deeper works of God.

Conversion: Almost or Altogether Christian?

Wesley lived in a "Christian" country, or at least a thoroughly "churched" one. Many people were religious, even if they did not have a personal relationship with God. They wanted to serve God, and Wesley had no desire to discourage such people. However, he understood that they were missing something. They were "Almost Christians," those—to quote one of Wesley's favorite verses on the subject—"having the form of godliness, but denying the power thereof" (2 Tim. 3:5*a*, KJV). Wesley describes this state as having the "faith of a servant," a partial conversion involving glimmers of understanding and the first stirrings of will but lacking something essential:

> The faith of a servant implies a divine evidence of the *invisible* and the *eternal* world; yea, and an evidence of the *spiritual world*, so far as it can exist without living experience. Whoever has attained this, the faith of a servant, "feareth God and escheweth evil"; or, as it is expressed by St. Peter, "feareth God and worketh righteousness." In consequence of which he is in a degree (as the Apostle observes), "accepted with him." Elsewhere he is described in those words, "He that feareth God, and keepeth his commandments." Even one who has gone thus far in religion, who obeys God out of fear, is not in any wise to be despised, seeing "the fear of the Lord is the beginning of wisdom." Nevertheless he should be exhorted not to stop there; not to

rest till he attains the adoption of sons; till he obeys out of love, which is the privilege of all the *children* of God.[10]

It is no surprise to see that love is what makes the difference between partial and full conversion. While obedience is important to Wesley, it finds its meaning within a context of love. Full conversion is defined by the move from an external, task-oriented approach to God to an internal, personal-relational approach. The goal of conviction and repentance is not to get the sinner to say, "I'm sorry for doing it wrong, God; I'll do better next time," as much as to say, "I'm sorry, Father, for having run away from you; I'm coming home now."

In the conclusion of his sermon "The Almost Christian," Wesley parses the difference between the "Almost Christian" and the "Altogether Christian" into three things, all of which enforce the relational character of salvation that is so typical of his theology.[11] The first mark of full conversion is a love for God. Love is what makes the difference between one who obeys God out of fear with the faith of a servant and one who obeys God joyfully as God's child. Second, this love for God must be joined to a love for everyone else (the "neighbor" of Jesus's Good Samaritan parable). "Almost Christians" might perform their religious duties for their own benefit, but "Altogether Christians" are as focused on loving others as God is on loving them. For Wesley, this love is not so much a feeling as an active disposition that is willing to sacrifice one's own good for the good of another. Third and lastly, the "Altogether Christian" has an active faith that is a "sure trust and confidence." The "Almost Christian" may be content to merely affirm truth, but the "Altogether Christian" always trusts God enough to act on it.

Given these lofty descriptions of full conversion, one might wonder if anyone has ever been fully converted. Wesley admits that the bar is set high, but he offers that mark as much as a trajectory of conversion as a single moment of it. To him, conversion is both a moment and a journey, a crisis and a process. To be a Christian is, in a sense, to be becoming a fuller Christian. Like so many other human relationships, our relationship with God is marked by single moments (like anniversaries) but mostly lived out between them. Our relationship with God is marked by the times when we decisively respond to God's grace in crisis moments, but it is lived out as a process of deeper conversion, a process of turning away from ourselves toward God and others.

When we act in response to God's prevenient grace, when we allow God to convert us, we invite God to act again. According to Wesley, there are two things that happen at that point, and they can be separated as concepts but never as events. One of these is something external, something that God does *for* us in the moment of our conversion, and Wesley, following the bulk of the Christian tradition, calls this justification. The other is something internal, something that God does *in* us. Wesley's favorite phrase to identify that is the "new birth," but for the purposes of comparison, we will label it initial sanctification. While both are important and necessary, Wesley sees the external work as a stepping-stone to the more important internal one.

Saving Grace: Justification and Initial Sanctification

The Protestant Reformation was, in some ways, a debate about the relationship between justification and sanctification. In that debate, the Protestants held up justification—especially justification by faith—as the primary reality, while the Catholics focused on sanctification as the key to salvation. Wesley saw the Methodists as distinctive because they valued both.

> It has been frequently observed that very few were clear in their judgment both with regard to justification and sanctification. . . . Who has wrote more ably than Martin Luther on justification by faith alone? And who was more ignorant of the doctrine of sanctification, or more confused in his conceptions of it? . . . On the other hand, how many writers of the Romish Church (as Francis Sales and Juan de Castaniza in particular) have wrote strongly and scripturally on sanctification; who nevertheless were entirely unacquainted with the nature of justification. . . . But it has pleased God to give the Methodists a full and clear knowledge of each, and the wide difference between them.[12]

This is a biased and oversimplified perspective, but the point Wesley makes here goes to the heart of his concerns about saving grace, the second step— indeed, the central step—in his *ordo salutis*. Wesley understands God to be doing two very different things when God "saves" a person. They both happen together, and they are as connected as two sides of the same coin. However, they are not the same work, and there is a clear logical priority between them.

Wesley articulates the difference between justification and initial sanctification or new birth as a difference between external realities and internal ones. In one sermon, he explains it this way:

> Justification implies only a relative, the new birth a real, change. God in justifying us does something *for* us: in begetting us again he does the work

in us. The former changes our outward relation to God, so that of enemies we become children; by the latter our inmost souls are changed, so that of sinners we become saints. The one restores us to the favour, the other to the image of God. The one is the taking away the guilt, the other the taking away the power, of sin.[13]

Logically speaking, the first of these works is the external one, and the priority Wesley gives to justification marks him as a Protestant. Our first problem is that we are guilty before God. Though we are not judged for Adam's sin, all of us have acted out our fallen condition and have incurred the displeasure and disfavor of God by our own violations of God's laws. By the time God helps us to realize our condition, we find ourselves out of favor with God and subject to God's wrath. So before any relationship can begin, we need to be forgiven, which is all that justification really is. As Wesley notes, "The plain scriptural notion of justification is pardon, the forgiveness of sins."[14]

Prevenient grace helps us understand this offer of forgiveness, but it only becomes effective when we trust God enough to accept the offer and to turn our lives over to God. Thus our justification becomes real *if* we have faith and *only if* we have faith. God offers a relationship, and relationships begin, not with the accomplishment of tasks, but merely with offers of mutual trust. God has made the first move, and all we have to do is respond to it. In that sense, faith is sufficient for salvation. If we will trust God, that's all we need. However, faith is all that we *can* have when we come to God. We bring no good deeds, and we cannot claim to earn God's forgiveness or pardon. There is no other starting point for our relationship with God, so faith is also necessary for salvation. If we will not trust God, then nothing else can help us.[15] Wesley learned this by his own experience leading up to Aldersgate.

The forgiveness that God offers in justification, however, is only the beginning. It is not the end—neither the finishing point nor the goal—of God's work. God wants to do more than declare sinners not guilty and make sure they do not end up in hell. And so, at the very moment that God justifies those who accept God's acceptance of them, God also begins the process of sanctifying them. God gives them a new birth and continues the processes of restoring God's image in them that God began with the first glimmerings of prevenient grace.

This is why Wesley liked the metaphor of a new birth. While faith is sufficient for justification, it is not sufficient for sanctification—some activity must be involved. New birth implies the beginning of a process of growth and development, not merely the end of one. One must be born in order to live, but the point of being born is not to stay an infant forever. Wesley puts the point another way, with a different metaphor, in one of his long, treatise-like letters, this one to Thomas Church. There he writes, "Our main doctrines, which include all the rest, are three—that of Repentance, of Faith, and of Holiness. The first of these we account, as it were, the porch of religion; the next, the door; the third, religion itself."[16]

Repentance is the work of prevenient grace, and the place to which we must come first if we are to get anywhere else. But standing on the porch is not entering the house. Faith is our response of trust to God's offer of a relationship, and that is what allows us to come in out of the cold, escaping God's wrath and entering into God's presence. This includes justification as the restoration of God's favor ("Yes, you may enter," God says) and also the new birth. But both of these events are only meaningful because they usher us into a new place. The point, the house itself, the very core of religion, was holiness, sanctification, the full renewal of the image of God that enables us to relate more and more deeply to God.

Wesley gives us a sense of the dynamic process of living out a spiritual life in his sermon "The New Birth." When someone is born again, Wesley says,

> All his spiritual senses are then "exercised to discern" spiritual "good and evil." By the use of these he is daily increasing in the knowledge of God, of Jesus Christ whom he hath sent, and of all the things pertaining to his inward kingdom. And now he may be properly said *to live*: God having quickened him by his Spirit, he is alive to God through Jesus Christ. He lives a life which the world knoweth not of, a "life" which "is hid with Christ in God." God is continually breathing, as it were, upon his soul, and his soul is breathing unto God. Grace is descending into his heart, and prayer and praise ascending to heaven. And by this intercourse between God and man, this fellowship with the Father and the Son, as by a kind of spiritual respiration, the life of God in the soul is sustained: and the child of God grows up, till he comes to "the full measure of the stature of Christ."[17]

So, though the new birth is the moment when living starts, it is not living itself. In Wesley's mind, living and relating to God is indistinguishable from growing and becoming like God. Just as justification is the necessary precondition for new birth, new birth is the precondition for sanctification, that ongoing renewal of God's image in us. It is to that third stage in Wesley's *ordo salutis* that we must now turn.

Sanctifying Grace: Perfecting in Love

The work of the Holy Spirit that is sanctifying grace is the core of salvation to Wesley. He will describe this work in various terms, most commonly "sanctification," "holiness," and "Christian perfection," but they all refer basically to the same thing—the deeper or more complete renewal of the image of God. Wesley takes great pains not to depreciate the work of saving grace, but he does not think God stops there. His ideas about sanctification reveal his radical optimism of grace, and they show just how high a bar God has set for God's self in the work of restoring humanity's true nature.

Sanctification as a Work of Grace

In our reflections on Wesley's understanding of *sanctifying* grace, it is important to keep in mind that it is a work of *grace* first and foremost. It is about what God does for us, not about what we do for ourselves. We have already encountered Wesley's dim view of "natural" human ability. Wesley's optimism of grace is anchored in the work of God and not in his estimation of human capacity. As above, God acts in sanctifying grace so that human beings can "re-act," but the priority must be given to God's work and not to humanity's response. Otherwise, the doctrine of Christian perfection easily slides into something like perfectionism, in which people focus on how holy they are rather than on how gracious God is. Wesley finds that attitude to be as detrimental to Christian holiness as any other of "Satan's devices."[18]

We should also remember that sanctifying grace describes God's restoration of our original created nature—the image of God. It is not about adding things to a human life that are somehow foreign or alien to it. Ultimately, God will make our destiny better than Eden, but in this life God's work is mostly about restoring what was lost in the fall. So we should not think of sanctification as God trying to create "supersaints," doing something out of place in ordinary human life. Because of the fall, we do not recognize that. What we naturally describe as a "full human life" is actually much less than that. God's sanctifying grace is really about God's helping us to become human again.

Sanctification and the Language of Perfection

Before we delve too far into Wesley's understanding of Christian perfection, we need to be clear on what he means by "perfect." The language of perfection is easily misunderstood, and Wesley often found himself defending and defining the idea. However, since the Bible used the language of perfection, Wesley was not about to give it up. He just tried to explain the biblical concept better.

Wesley usually confronts misunderstandings about perfection by talking about what it is not. In these discussions, we see Wesley trying to be as realistic about human capacity as he is optimistic about God's grace. Our human condition is always one of limitation, and so any perfection we can attain will never involve perfect performance. In his sermon "On Perfection," Wesley puts it this way:

> The highest perfection which man can attain while the soul dwells in the body does not exclude ignorance and error, and a thousand other infirmities. Now from wrong judgments wrong words and actions will often necessarily flow. . . . Nor can I be freed from a liableness to such a mistake while I remain in a corruptible body. A thousand infirmities in consequence of this will attend my spirit till it returns to God who gave it. And in numberless instances it comes short of doing the will of God as Adam did in paradise. Hence the best of men may say from the heart,
>
> Every moment, Lord, I need
> The merit of thy death.[19]

The fact that we will never perform perfectly also helps us to realize that Christian perfection is never an "independent" perfection. Holiness never exempts one from a reliance on Christ and a faith in his atonement. We do not receive it from God and walk away, as if God were to say, "I'm finished with you now. You are perfect; move along." As Wesley notes in his *Plain Account of Christian Perfection,*

> The holiest of men still need Christ as their Prophet, as "the light of the world." For he does not give them light, but from moment to moment; the instant he withdraws, all is darkness. They still need Christ as their King. For God does not give them a stock of holiness. But unless they receive a supply every moment, nothing but unholiness would remain. They still need Christ as their Priest, to make atonement for their holy things. Even perfect holiness is acceptable to God only through Jesus Christ.[20]

This is the reason why Wesley wanted to avoid the phrase "sinless perfection." It was not completely erroneous given his careful definition of sin, but it led to misunderstandings. As he notes in one of his letters: *"Sinless perfection?* Neither do I contend *for this,* seeing the term is not scriptural. A perfection that perfectly fulfils the whole law, and so needs not the merits of Christ? I acknowledge none such—I do now, and always did, protest against it."[21]

So Christian perfection does not mean perfect knowledge, perfect performance, or a place where God is finished working in us. We never get to the point where we no longer need to pray "Forgive us our trespasses," nor do we outgrow our reliance on the atoning blood of Christ. But if perfection is not this static ideal, then what is it? To Wesley, it was a dynamic concept related to the way he understood the perfection of God's original creation, and it was a concept that was ultimately grounded not in performance but in love.

Sanctification and Dynamic, Perfect Love

As we saw in Wesley's thoughts on creation, Wesley's concept of perfection and goodness was dynamic. Perfection was not so much "as good as possible ever" but "as good as possible for now and still improving." No matter how good a created thing might be, it is still possible for God to make it even better. Wesley knew that the biblical language of perfection was tied to the idea of maturity, and maturity is always a moving target. Mature behavior in a five-year-old may be immature behavior in a ten-year-old. Even as adults, most of us realize we still have some growing up to do. This is how Wesley wants us to understand the language of perfection, particularly as it is tied to the work of sanctifying grace. In summing up the ways perfection is often misunderstood, Wesley has this to say:

> Yet we may, lastly, observe that neither in this respect is there any absolute perfection on earth. There is no "perfection of degrees," as it is termed; none which does not admit of a continual increase. So that how much soever any man hath attained, or in how high a degree soever he is perfect, he hath still need to "grow in grace," and daily to advance in the knowledge and love of God his Saviour.[22]

This dynamic view of perfection is tied to Wesley's understanding of what makes something good in the first place. Something is good when it fits in well in the place it was designed to fit, doing what it was designed to do. So when we use the language of perfection on human beings, we have to remind ourselves what human beings were created for. God created humanity in God's image so that human beings could relate to God and each other. Relationship is the goal of human living, and so the "goodness" of human beings is found in their ability to relate. Perfection, then, is found in those who relate as well as they can at that moment. Since we know that the fundamental quality of personal relationships is love, we might be tempted to simply define Christian perfection as perfect love. And, of course, this is exactly what Wesley does.

Over and over again, throughout his writing, Wesley will define the intertwining concepts of sanctification, holiness, and Christian perfection in terms of love, more specifically a love for God that always results in a love for one's neighbor as well. In his sermon "On Perfection," he sums up the concept like this:

> What is then the perfection of which man is capable while he dwells in a corruptible body? It is the complying with that kind command, "My son, give me thy heart." It is the "loving the Lord his God with all his heart, and with all his soul, and with all his mind." This is the sum of Christian perfection: it is all comprised in that one word, love. The first branch of it is the love of God: and as he that loves God loves his brother also, it is inseparably connected with the second, "Thou shalt love thy neighbour as thyself." Thou shalt love every man as thy own soul, as Christ loved us. "On these two commandments hang all the law and the prophets": these contain the whole of Christian perfection.[23]

Loving relationship was what human beings were created for; it was the whole reason God implanted God's image in us. This is what was lost in the fall, and with it all true human happiness. But love is exactly what all grace eventually aims at restoring. The priority of love in his thought explains why Wesley thinks that full salvation demands more than justification. The sinful acts that make both us and others miserable all flow out of our unloving nature. Merely forgiving them does not fix the fundamental problem. In Wesley's eyes, God is not content to combat only the symptoms of our selfish will by constantly forgiving all of the sins that arise from it. God wants to fully heal our diseased will so that it is driven by nothing but love, nothing but a desire for God and for the good of everyone else around us. The full reorientation of that will would then be worthy of being called entire sanctification.

The Question of Entire Sanctification

There is probably no part of Wesley's thought that has been as thoroughly discussed and explored by his theological descendants as entire sanctification. Though Wesley himself did not use the phrase "entire sanctification" very often (he preferred the phrase "full salvation"), he did affirm that the work of sanctification is something God can do "entirely" in this life. The mechanics of the work, however, are not so clear. Even in his own time, Wesley was aware of the debate about how God performed God's sanctifying work. There were some who claimed that God's work was a gradual process that could—though it did not always—culminate in a finished work. There were others who claimed that God's work was better described as an instantaneous crisis-like moment in which all that God was going to do was accomplished at once. Wesley's answer, like so many of his theological positions, was that both were true in their own ways, and he held the two in tension.

To begin with, Wesley himself felt that the debate about processes and crises would always exist because Scripture itself was not clear on the issue. This made Wesley focus on the fact of sanctification more than he argued about its manner. In preaching "On Patience," he said,

> But it may be inquired, In what manner does God work this entire, this universal change in the soul of the believer? . . . Does he work it gradually, by slow degrees? Or instantaneously, in a moment? How many are the disputes upon this head, even among the children of God! And so there will be, after all that ever was or ever can be said upon it. . . . And they will be the more resolute herein because the Scriptures are silent upon the subject. . . . Every man therefore may abound in his own sense, provided he will allow the same liberty to his neighbour. . . . Permit me likewise to add one more thing. Be the change instantaneous or gradual, see that you never rest till it is wrought in your own soul, if you desire to dwell with God in glory.[24]

As a pastor, Wesley is more concerned that people experience God's work than that they describe it well, and so he focuses on seeking this full work of God no matter how it comes. But having said that, Wesley's personal opinion—which he gives his readers permission to take or leave as they will—is that the work of entire sanctification is better described as an instantaneous one than a gradual one.

Wesley's primary reason for asserting this is that the testimonies he has heard—and interestingly, Wesley does not add himself to this number—all affirm that God worked this fullness of love instantly in the individuals' hearts. An instantaneous view of sanctification also reinforces the idea that it is God's work, not something we work toward. In justification, God forgives us in a moment. In entire sanctification, God fills our hearts with God's love. Since God's work requires no prerequisites, God can work it immediately. Wesley outlines that simple logic like this: "1) that Christian perfection is that love of God and our neighbour which implies deliverance from *all sin*; 2) that this is received merely *by faith;* 3) that it is given *instantaneously,* in one moment; 4) that we are to expect it (not at death, but) *every moment*—that *now* is the accepted time, *now* is the day of this salvation."[25]

Of course, this does not mean that God expects people to idly wait around after justification for God to sanctify them. Just as prevenient grace engages people in a process that results in a moment of conversion, so, too, sanctifying grace creates a process that leads people to the moment of entire sanctification. Here, Wesley finds the analogy between "dying out to self" and actual physical death to be a helpful one. In answer to the question, "Is this death to sin, and renewal in love, gradual or instantaneous?" Wesley replies,

> A man may be *dying* for some time; yet he does not, properly speaking, *die* till the instant the soul is separated from the body. And in that instant he lives the life of eternity. In like manner he may be *dying to sin* for some time; yet he is not "dead to sin" till sin is separated from his soul. And in that instant he lives the full life of love. . . . Yet he stills grows in grace, in the knowledge of Christ, in the love and image of God; and will do so, not only till death, but to all eternity.[26]

That process of dying to self is not a passive waiting but an active engagement. The very next question in *A Plain Account of Christian Perfection* is this: "How are we to wait for this change?" Wesley's response shows his awareness of how God connects divine activity with our own:

> Not in careless indifference or indolent inactivity, but in vigorous, universal obedience, in a zealous keeping of all the commandments, in watchfulness and painfulness, in denying ourselves and taking up our cross daily; as well as in earnest prayer and fasting, and a close attendance on all the ordinances of God. And if any man dream of attaining it any other way (yea, or of *keeping* it when it is attained, when he has received it, even in the largest measure) he deceiveth his own soul. 'Tis true, we receive it by simple faith. But God does not, will not, give that faith, unless we seek it with all diligence in the way which he hath ordained.[27]

So, then, the saving work of God is an instantaneous gift, but God tends only to give it to those who are actively engaged in a process of seeking and waiting. And this is what Wesley is constantly exhorting his people to do. "Do all that you can," he seems to say, "and you will find in so doing that God does all that God can as well."

This, then, is Wesley's view of salvation. It is about God's grace restoring to us our capacities to love and relate, restoring God's image in us. Prevenient grace opens the door by awakening our understanding and our will. If we choose to respond to God, God restores us to God's full favor and then begins the process of equipping us with more and more of God's character so that we can love God more deeply and share God's love with our neighbor. The goal is for God to so fill our hearts with love that there is simply no room for anything else. If we continue with God in this journey, then the unfolding of ever deeper relationships will be the work of all eternity. However, if we choose to refuse God's offers and walk away from God, God will respect that choice as well. This, of course, would be the highest tragedy, and one Wesley was constantly and urgently pleading with his hearers and readers to avoid, but it is still possible.

However, if salvation is all about love and relationship, then salvation cannot—by its very nature—be something that happens to isolated individuals or something that is merely "between me and God." Love implies community, and so, to finish our exploration of Wesley's thought, we will turn to his understanding of church and of all those communal and social factors that influence and shape our life with God.

fourteen
Wesley's Thoughts on the Church

---

*O*ne might be tempted to think that, with his thoughts on Christian perfection, we have already reached the pinnacle of Wesley's beliefs, the highest expression of salvation to be found in this life. Certainly people talk about Wesley in those terms. Many books and sermons have held up individual entire sanctification as if it were God's ultimate goal. Such a view, however, misses the essentially relational nature of Wesley's approach to salvation. Even sanctification is instrumental in Wesley's mind, a step on the road to somewhere else. God does not save people just so that they might be sanctified. God saves and sanctifies people so that they might be empowered to love—and love is not something that can exist in an individual alone. The peak of Wesley's doctrine of salvation is, therefore, not individual entire sanctification; it is a community in which people who are being entirely sanctified (however far along they may be) express their God-given love for one another and extend that love beyond the community into the world. In Wesley's mind, the "way to heaven" is not traveled alone. The way God connects to us cannot be separated from the way God connects us to each other. This brings us to Wesley's thoughts on the church.

There are four features of Wesley's understanding of church and Christian community that we will explore in this chapter. Each of these intuitions had a profound shape on Wesley's own life and ministry, and they continue to be useful to life and ministry today. First, we will explore some of Wesley's thoughts on the essentially communal nature of the Christian religion, connecting his thoughts on church to his thoughts on God, humanity, and the drama of salvation. In Wesley's mind, there is no such thing as an independent Christian.

Second, we will look more deeply at the nature of Christian community. For Wesley, the church was, at its heart, a group of believers bound together by God's love as administered through the Holy Spirit. Christian communities are essentially communities of love. This makes Wesley's view of church inherently ecumenical, since he strongly affirms that things such as doctrinal agreement or common worship practices are secondary and should never be allowed to get in the way of love.

Third, we will examine how, in Wesley's mind, this community united in love is first and foremost a community of purpose and action, a "missional" community, to use more contemporary language. Certainly we do not have to perform good deeds in order to begin to relate to God—God offers us God's love through grace. But once begun, our relationship with God can only be expressed in obedience and action. The love that Wesley refers to is not a feeling, as if the church were a social club that gets together because people enjoy it. Instead, Wesley understands "love" as an action word. The church is the primary physical embodiment of God's love in the world, and the church's mission is to take part in God's activity in the world. Wesley's idea of church, then, is more concerned with function than with form. All of the church's forms—its traditions, modes of worship, organizational structures, and the like—must serve its function, its mission. Wesley's entire life and ministry lived out this conviction. He ignored old forms that no longer fit the mission, and he created new ones—such as his class meetings or lay preaching—as he saw the Holy Spirit empowering the church to fulfill its mission in new times and circumstances.

Finally, we will explore how the mission of the church includes those outside of it. Since God's love encompasses all of humankind, the church's expression of that love must do the same. The church's most obvious work is the spiritual support of its members, but its task is much larger. It is just as much a part of the church's life to extend God's love to the world, meeting the physical needs of people in compassionate ministry and sharing the gospel in evangelism.

Christianity as a Communal Religion

Wesley's understanding of God is anchored in his idea that God is love. "Thy nature, and thy name, is LOVE," as Charles Wesley put it in a hymn.[1] God creates human beings in God's image so that they, too, could be capable of giving and receiving love. Human beings disrupt their loving relationships with God and each other by focusing on themselves, and so sin represents the antithesis of love—a selfish focus over an "other focus." God's salvation, from the free gift of faith and justification in Christ to the sanctifying work of the Holy Spirit, is all about repairing the damage done by sin and restoring the capacities for love and relationship. It is, therefore, impossible for this kind of salvation to be given to isolated individuals, and Wesley is fully aware of these implications.

Reflecting on Jesus's claim that his followers were the "salt of the earth" (Matt. 5:13, KJV), Wesley connects his relational intuitions about God and humanity to Christianity and the church. "Christianity is essentially a social religion," Wesley writes, "and that to turn it into a solitary religion is indeed to destroy it."[2] By "essentially" here, Wesley does not just mean "basically" but actually "in essence." It is the social nature of Christianity that makes it the religion that it is, and if one were to take that away, what would be left could not be considered Christianity.

Wesley goes into a fuller explanation of the essentially social nature of Christianity in the preface he wrote to the compilation *Hymns and Sacred Poems* back in the earliest days of the Evangelical Revival (1739). In that preface, he describes what he calls the "mystical" ideal of Christianity, in which the highest goal of religion is the solitary contemplation of the divine Being in a kind of inward stillness, with no one else around and without doing anything directed to the outside. After summarizing that view, he has this to say:

> Directly opposite to this is the gospel of Christ. Solitary religion is not to be found there. "Holy solitaries" is a phrase no more consistent with the gospel than holy adulterers. The gospel of Christ knows of no religion, but social; no holiness but social holiness. "Faith working by love" is the length and breadth and depth and height of Christian perfection. "This commandment have we from Christ, that he who loves God, love his brother also"; and that we manifest our love "by doing good unto all men; especially to them that are of the household of faith." And in truth, whosoever loveth his brethren, not in word only, but as Christ loved him, cannot but be "zealous of good works." He feels in his soul a burning, restless desire, of spending and being spent for them. "My Father," will he say, "worketh hitherto, and I work." And at all possible opportunities he is, like his Master, "going about doing good."[3]

The highest expression of Christianity is not an inward holiness that makes the soul glow but an outward loving-by-doing directed at fellow believers and the world. A community of faith is not merely a helpful addition to one's spiritual life, as if one could make it on one's own but it is just easier with other people. Rather, it is the only place where one can live one's faith out.

Early on in his life, Wesley understood that believers advance their faith and progress toward full salvation by their connection with other believers. We see it in the Holy Club at Oxford and in his small groups in Georgia, but it reaches its fullest expression in the Methodist societies. In *A Plain Account of the People Called Methodists*, Wesley talks about the need for mutual support among the first converts of the Evangelical Revival.

> They wanted to "flee from the wrath to come," and to assist each other in so doing. They therefore united themselves "in order to pray together, to receive the word of exhortation, and to watch over one another in love, that they might help each other to work out their salvation." . . .
>
> They now likewise agreed that as many of them as had opportunity would meet together every Friday, and spend the dinner hour in crying to God, both for each other and for all mankind.
>
> . . . In a few months the far greater part of those who had begun to "fear God and work righteousness," but were not united together, grew faint in their minds, and fell back into what they were before. Meanwhile the far greater part of those who were thus united together continued "striving to enter in at the strait gate," and to "lay hold on eternal life."
>
> Upon reflection I could not but observe, This is the very thing which was from the beginning of Christianity.[4]

In this spontaneous association, Wesley saw a return to the root of what Christianity was all about. The Holy Spirit led the individual converts to come together to help each other on the path of salvation. They were even praying for those who had not yet begun the journey, since their prayers were not only for each other but also "for all mankind." This society was open to anyone who wanted salvation, regardless of what they believed at the time or how they might prefer to worship. Its focus was mutual support in the spiritual life. As Wesley observed this fledgling group, it was community that made the difference between those who persevered in their faith and those who fell away.

Wesley knew that faith was a personal reality, but he also knew that personal faith must have an interpersonal context to flourish and grow. The formation of Methodist societies was a practical application of Wesley's relational theology, and it marked the effective difference between Wesley's wing of the Evangelical Revival and the others. George Whitefield recognized this. His ministry was focused on individual conversions and not on the formation of communities, but this made his people only a "rope of sand," a bunch of individual pieces with nothing that bound them together. Wesley's attention to Christian community is, therefore, a matter of both consistent theology and effective practice, and something we should pay careful attention to as well.

Church as Community of Love

As we have seen, what bound Wesley's communities together was not a set of common ideas but more a common goal of salvation. However, Wesley does not attribute the unity of these communities to their members' determination or strength. Like everything having to do with salvation, Wesley understood that the common goal of salvation was rooted in the common love and faith that they shared, which were gracious gifts of God. A God-given unity in faith and love becomes Wesley's essential definition of what it means to be a church. In his sermon "Of the Church," written late in his life as a summary of his mature reflections on the matter, Wesley makes the following claim:

Here then is a clear unexceptionable answer to that question, What is the church? The catholic or universal church is all the persons in the universe whom God hath so called out of the world as to entitle them to the preceding character; as to be "one body," united by "one spirit"; having "one faith, one hope, one baptism; one God and Father of all, who is above all, and through all, and in them all."[5]

Using Paul's language in Ephesians, Wesley defines church in terms of the action of God and of Christian unity. God acts to give faith and to empower repentance and holy living, and this becomes the foundation of the church. God's act to call people out of the world at the same time calls them into a family united together under God as Father. It is God who unites believers as a church, not their doctrinal agreement or their common worship practices. Wesley demonstrates the priority of love in this unity over doctrine and forms of worship by the way he works out the ecumenical implications of his definition.

Wesley cites the Church of England's definition of "church": "The visible church of Christ is a congregation of faithful men, in which the pure word of God is preached, and the sacraments be duly administered."[6] He heartily endorses the first part of that definition, particularly if one understands the "congregation of faithful men" as referring to a true, relational, trust-in-God kind of faith. But when the definition adds qualifications about doctrine and practice, Wesley has a problem. He writes,

> I will not undertake to defend the accuracy of this definition. I dare not exclude from the church catholic all those congregations in which any un-scriptural doctrines which cannot be affirmed to be "the pure word of God" are sometimes, yea, frequently preached. Neither all those congregations in which the sacraments are not "duly administered." . . . I can easily bear with their holding wrong opinions, yea, and superstitious modes of worship. Nor would I on these accounts scruple still to include them within the pale of the catholic church. Neither would I have any objection to receive them, if they desired it, as members of the Church of England.[7]

Wesley seems to think that God's work in bringing people together does not depend on proper doctrine or good practice. It is not that these are unimportant. Wesley unashamedly labels some of these opinions "wrong" and some of the practices "superstitious." The bulk of Wesley's writings across his lifetime speak of his concern to promote good ideas and practices and to critique bad ones. So those things must be important to Wesley. They are just not essential, not nearly as important as Christians displaying genuine love for one another and for the world.

We can see Wesley's focus on love as the essence of church in his insistence that right theological opinions (orthodoxy) are not the essence of religion and in his deliberate efforts to extend the hand of fellowship across doctrinal boundary lines. One of Wesley's most controversial statements was his claim "that *ortho-doxy*, or *right opinions*, is at best but a very slender *part* of religion, if it can be allowed to be any part of it at all."[8] In later defending this claim in a letter to Bishop Warburton of Gloucester, Wesley goes on to say this:

> After premising that it is our bounden duty to labour after a *right judg-ment* in all things, as a *wrong judgment* naturally leads to wrong *practice*, I say again, *right opinion* is at best but a very *slender part* of religion (which properly and directly consists in right tempers, words, and actions) and frequently it is *no part* of religion. For it may be where there is no religion at all: in men of the most abandoned lives; yea, in the devil himself.[9]

Wesley affirms that right judgments are important but only because better judgments lead to better practices. It is, however, the practices that matter. It is the activities (words and actions) by which our love expresses itself and the fount from which those activities spring (tempers) that is the real heart of religion for

Wesley. Disconnected from such things, right opinions are worthless. Even the devil has those.[10]

Because of this attitude, Wesley found it important to seek unity with all who claimed to be disciples of Christ, no matter how they understood their faith. In the church, he called this priority of faith working in love the "catholic spirit." His sermon with that phrase as its title is a plea for Christians to love one another and not to let differences in doctrine or practice divide them. He recognized that divisions among Christians made it hard for the church to function as a community of love to those on the inside and as an example and extension of love to those on the outside. Here Wesley sets down his clearest affirmation of the priority of love in the church over all else.

Taking his cue from the encounter between Jehu and Jehonadab in 2 Kings 10, Wesley picks up the idea that if our hearts are united, then our hands should be also. He is realistic that there will always be institutional differences between Christians, but he does not want them to have the final word.

> But although a difference in opinions or modes of worship may prevent an entire external union, yet need it prevent our union in affection? Though we can't think alike, may we not love alike? May we not be of one heart, though we are not of one opinion? Without all doubt we may. Herein all the children of God may unite, notwithstanding these smaller differences. These remaining as they are, they may forward one another in love and in good works.[11]

Even when Wesley is convinced that some of the opinions people hold are outright damaging to faith—as he is with some of the specific beliefs of Roman Catholicism—he still does not see that as reason enough to withhold the hand of fellowship. In a rather remarkable move for an eighteenth-century Anglican—and one for which he knows he will be criticized—Wesley writes a letter to "a Roman Catholic" in which he summarizes the barest essentials of Christian belief and then pleads,

> Are we not thus far agreed? Let us thank God for this, and receive it as a fresh token of his love. But if God still loveth us, we ought also to love one another. We ought, without this endless jangling about opinions, to provoke one another to love and to good works. Let the points wherein we differ stand aside; here are enough wherein we agree, enough to be the ground of every Christian temper and of every Christian action.

. . . Then, if we cannot as yet think alike in all things, at least we may love alike. Herein we cannot possibly do amiss. For of one point none can doubt a moment,—"God is love; and he that dwelleth in love, dwelleth in God, and God in him."[12]

God's love—first accepted then reexpressed—is what binds the church together. To build on any other foundation, Wesley thinks, is useless. And love is, by nature, active. If the church really is a community of purpose, and if the love that Wesley pleads for actually becomes present, it will inevitably drive the church into action.

The Church's Mission as Active Love

One of the simple ways that psychologists classify personalities is with the distinction between task orientation and person orientation. Up to this point, Wesley's church looks as if it has a more person-oriented personality than a task-oriented one, and this would fit with the relational focus of his entire theology and his strong emphasis on love. However, as with so many things about Wesley's theology, Wesley is good at combining things with a both-and approach that other people tend to separate with an either-or approach. In the case of the church, the emphasis on love and person drives a concern for mission and task. Wesley knows no other kind of love than an active love. His theology is oriented toward people, but people relate to one another by doing things. This makes mission and activity just as much a part of the church's identity as love. Wesley puts it this way:

It is most true that the root of religion lies in the heart, in the inmost soul; that this is the union of the soul with God, the life of God in the soul of man. But if this root be really in the heart it cannot but put forth branches. And these are the several instances of outward obedience, which partake of the same nature with the root, and consequently, are not only marks or signs, but substantial parts of religion. . . .

. . . It is granted that the love of God and man arising from "faith unfeigned" is all in all "the fulfilling of the law." . . . But it does not follow, that love is all [in all] in such a sense as to supersede either faith or good works. It is "the fulfilling of the law," not by releasing us from but by constraining us to obey it. It is "the end of the commandment" as every commandment leads to and centres in it.[13]

For Wesley, inward religion *always* results in outward obedience, which is why he claimed that certain forms of obedience were just as much a part of religion as the relationship to God that drove them. Love is, indeed, everything, but only by encompassing all good works, not by replacing them. If the activity of love is lacking, we have every reason to doubt its presence.

The activity of love, then, is the mission, the primary task, of the church. To put it more specifically, the church is supposed to be the communal context that nurtures the fullest exercise of love, both for God and for other human beings. *Its* job is to help its individual members do *their* job of loving. Wesley makes these connections explicit in his sermon "On Zeal," where he describes religion as a series of concentric circles, the innermost being love and the outmost being the church.

> In a Christian believer *love* sits upon the throne, which is erected in the inmost soul; namely, love of God and man, which fills the whole heart, and reigns without a rival. In a circle near the throne are all *holy tempers*: long-suffering, gentleness, meekness, goodness, fidelity, temperance—and if any other is comprised in "the mind which was in Christ Jesus." In an exterior circle are all the *works of mercy*, whether to the souls or bodies of men. By these we exercise all holy tempers; by these we continually improve them, so that all these are real *means of grace*, although this is not commonly adverted to. Next to these are those that are usually termed *works of piety*: reading and hearing the Word, public, family, private prayer, receiving the Lord's Supper, fasting or abstinence. Lastly, that his followers may the more effectually provoke one another to love, holy tempers, and good works, our blessed Lord has united them together in one—*the church*, dispersed all over the earth; a little emblem of which, of the church universal, we have in every particular Christian congregation.
>
> This is that religion which our Lord has established upon earth, ever since the descent of the Holy Ghost on the day of Pentecost. This is the entire, connected system of Christianity: and thus the several parts of it rise one above another, from that lowest point, "the assembling ourselves together," to the highest, love enthroned in the heart.[14]

This quote is illuminating for several reasons, not the least of which is the clear priority Wesley gives to works of mercy (what we might call compassionate ministry) over works of piety. We will take up that crucial aspect of the church's mission in the next section, however. For now, we should note that the church is both the final expression of love as it filters through holy tempers to works of mercy and piety and the servant of all those things. Love naturally gives rise to tempers that give rise to activity that gives rise to a community of activity, but the purpose of this community is to empower those realities that gave it birth. The Lord "united them together" in order to "more effectively provoke one another" to have love and express it properly.

Wesley will go on in that sermon to exhort his readers to be zealous for the church but only if they are willing to be more zealous for the works of piety, even more zealous for works of mercy, and more zealous still for holy tempers and to reserve their "choicest zeal" for love alone. "The church," he writes, "the ordinances, outward works of every kind, yea, all other holy tempers, are inferior to this, and rise in value only as they approach nearer and nearer to it."[15] The mission of the church is to be an agent and promoter of love. We gather together in order to act on our love for one another and to empower each other to love even more. Our works of piety—our public prayers and sermons and taking of the Lord's Supper—are important as means by which our love for God and neighbor is increased but only important for that reason. Any other use of them is a misuse of them.

It is in this light that we should read all of the controversy over Wesley's engagement with the various forms of church activity, either because he ignored ones that others thought important (such as the parish boundary system) or because he created new forms that had no place in the old system (such as field preaching or lay preaching). Any means by which the church tried to promote works of piety or mercy had to be evaluated by how well it served the church's mission of empowering love. Love knew no political boundaries, so Wesley felt free to ignore them. When church doors shut out God's love, Wesley preached outside of them. If official Anglican priests were not really helping people learn to love God and neighbor, Wesley would find people who would—whether or not they had university degrees or the church's ordination. Form followed function, as far as Wesley was concerned. The mission governed everything, and that mission was all about love.

Wesley's focus on love, however, does not mean that forms of institutional organization or worship were irrelevant. Remember that Wesley was, at least in his own mind, a dyed-in-the-wool Anglican. He instinctively resisted those various changes we discussed above until he was convinced that they were, in fact, serving the church's mission. His basic attitude toward institutional forms was, therefore, very conservative. He assumed that you should not change anything unless and until it proved itself useless or something better had come along. And so, for example, he did not want his Methodists to separate institutionally from the Church of England because there was no need to do so. He encouraged his Methodists to attend Church of England services as well as their society meetings because God was, indeed, using both of those means to build them up in love.[16] When the Church of England would not ordain sufficient ministers for America, Wesley did not say that ordination did not matter. He simply convinced himself (for good or for ill) that he had as much power to ordain ministers as any Anglican bishop might. And even though he saw, for example, the Lord's Supper as a means to the higher end of love, he still found it an indispensable means and encouraged his people to take Communion as often as they possibly could.[17] Wesley, thus, was not a Quaker, ready to throw away all liturgy and sacrament because spiritual things were more important. The means by which the church fulfilled its mission of promoting love were important to him. They were just not as important as the love they were designed to promote and had to be judged against that standard.

There was one part of that mission of promoting love, however, that could not be fulfilled inside the church, no matter what form one created, because it involved those who were outside of it. And so we will conclude our look at Wesley's thoughts on the church by looking at how the church was supposed to love those who were not yet a part of it.

The Church's Mission as Love Extended

There is an interesting tension in Wesley's view of the church, a tension between a church that exists as a context of love for its members and a church that exists to extend God's love into the world. On the one hand, Wesley frequently echoes what he feels to be the biblical priority for those in the church to take care of their fellow believers. So, for example, he interprets Jesus's words in Matthew 25:40 ("Inasmuch as ye have done it unto one of the least of these my brethren, ye have done it unto me" [KJV]) as referring to Christians and comments, "What encouragement is here to assist the household of faith?"[18] On the other hand, Wesley is also constantly seeking to widen that focus to include those outside the church as well, and so he continues his comment on that same verse by saying, "But let us likewise remember to do good to all men."[19]

This is an important tension to recognize because many churches today still face it. Some want to focus on discipleship among their members, while others want to focus on social justice issues such as poverty fighting or peacemaking. Here again we find Wesley trying to hold both attitudes together. Wesley's allows love to begin inside the church, but it must eventually move beyond it. One of Wesley's favorite verses to quote was Galatians 6:10 ("As we have therefore opportunity, let us do good unto all men, especially unto them who are of the household of faith" [KJV]). Interestingly, Wesley most often only cites the first half of the verse. The addendum Paul adds ("especially unto them who are of the household of faith") is one that Wesley usually—though not always—drops.[20]

Given Wesley's view of human beings as "embodied spirits," we would expect Wesley to understand doing "good unto all" in both spiritual and physical terms. In his own life and ministry, Wesley always tried to balance these two, and he encouraged his Methodists to do the same. He spent his life traveling and sharing the gospel as he understood it, and he spent his means trying to help the poor. He includes among those "works of mercy" whatever affects both bodies and souls. He encouraged his Methodists to share the gospel with their neighbors[21] as well as meet their physical needs. In his sermon "On Visiting the Sick," Wesley encourages his Methodists to attend to any who are afflicted in any way, first inquiring about their physical needs and then—and only then—helping to point them to God.[22] In Wesley's mind, the physical and the spiritual can never truly be separated, and so loving one's neighbors always includes seeking the good of their bodies as well as the good of their souls.

With that balance in mind, however, we should also note that Wesley felt that loving people and meeting their physical needs was not merely a means of getting to the more important spiritual matters. While he unashamedly believed that spiritual values were higher, he would not let the lack of spiritual outcomes be an excuse for ignoring physical needs. In discussing what it means for the church to be "salt and light" in the world, Wesley addresses those who would dismiss the value of compassionate ministry. Some would say that it was unimportant because spiritual needs were more important than physical ones. Others were frustrated because meeting people's physical needs did not always produce spiritual fruit or lead them to join the church. Wesley's answer to both of these objections was stark and unapologetic, and it provides a nice summary of the ideas he had about how the mission of the church connects to the work of God in the world.

I answer, (1), whether they will finally be lost or saved, you are expressly commanded to feed the hungry and clothe the naked. If you can and do not, whatever becomes of them, you shall go away into everlasting fire. (2). Though it is God only changes hearts, yet he generally doth it by man. It is our part to do all that in us lies as diligently as if we could change them ourselves, and then to leave the event to him. (3). God, in answer to their prayers, builds up his children by each other in every good gift, nourishing and strengthening the whole "body by that which every joint supplieth."[23]

So our love for God results in our obedience, and that is something we do regardless of how "successful" we might be in the tasks God asks us to perform. "Unsuccessful" obedience also gives the opportunity to practice being like Jesus. Just a bit later, Wesley continues:

It is very possible this fact also may be true, that you have tried to do good and have not succeeded; yea, that those who seemed reformed relapsed into sin, and their last state was worse than the first. And what marvel? Is the servant above his master? But how often did he strive to save sinners! And they would not hear; or when they had followed him awhile they turned back as a dog to his vomit. But he did not therefore desist from striving to do good. No more should you, whatever your success be. It is your part to do as you are commanded: the event is in the hand of God. You are not accountable for this.[24]

This, then, is how Wesley understood the church and its work. Our salvation is a communal thing because both God and human beings are communal and relational. For this reason, God gathers God's followers together into a church. This church is first and foremost a family bound together in love and not an institution united by doctrinal or practical agreement. This family, however, is an active one. Love is a verb, and it is expressed both by what we do in the church for God and others and by the ways we reach out to those beyond it. And as that dynamic of love flows from God and through human beings, God's kingdom goes forward. People are renewed after God's image in sanctification, and God's will is done on "earth, as it is in heaven" (Matt. 6:10, KJV).

The church engages in the task of sharing God's love with the world regardless of whether or not the world will respond. In that way, they simply love as God loves, which is fitting for a community being renewed in God's image. The church works toward God's kingdom, but it does not pretend to bring it about. That is God's work and God's alone. What God requires of the church at work in the world is simply the joyful obedience that naturally arises from love. The results are all in God's hands. Wesley admits that love is not always effective, but that is no excuse to stop loving. One simply loves because God is love. One seeks the good of even sinners because that's what Jesus sought. Love, in that sense, is its own end. That is how God works, and that is how God expects God's church to work as well.

Conclusion

We have now explored the outlines of John Wesley's world, the central events that shaped his life and the basic intuitions that shaped his thought. Since the task of a good introduction is as much to raise good questions as answer them, we will finish in full awareness of how unfinished our task is. There are two main trajectories the readers of Wesley could take upon finishing this book, and they are by no means mutually exclusive. One is the academic trajectory for those who wish to learn more about John Wesley. The other is the practical trajectory concerning what we do with all this stuff now that we have it on the table. We will try to give the reader a brief orientation to each.

For Further Study . . .

As we noted at the start of this journey, this book is only an attempt to introduce the reader to the riches of John Wesley's theological legacy. There are many writers who have explored that legacy with much greater depth and insight. Now that we have been introduced to Wesley, we can continue our journey with him in a number of different ways. For other short introductions to Wesley that have different orientations and perspectives, readers can explore William J. Abraham's *Wesley for Armchair Theologians* (Louisville, KY: Westminster-John Knox, 2005) and Jason E. Vickers's *Wesley: A Guide for the Perplexed* (New York: T and T Clark, 2009).

For those interested in more biographical reading, Kenneth J. Collins's *John Wesley: A Theological Journey* (Nashville: Abingdon, 2003), Richard Heitzenrater's *The Elusive Mr. Wesley* (Nashville: Abingdon, 2003), and Henry D. Rack's *Reasonable Enthusiast: John Wesley and the Rise of Methodism* (Nashville: Abingdon, 1993) are good places to start. Older but still useful is the work of Martin

177

Schmidt (*John Wesley: A Theological Biography*, trans. Norman P. Goldhawk [New York: Abingdon, 1963]).

Those who would like deeper engagement with Wesley's thought—books that bring out different facets of his work and focus on different concerns— would do well to read both Randy L. Maddox's *Responsible Grace: John Wesley's Practical Theology* (Nashville: Kingswood, 1994) and Kenneth J. Collins's *The Theology of John Wesley: Holy Love and the Shape of Grace* (Nashville: Abingdon, 2007). Shorter but also very helpful are Theodore Runyon's *The New Creation: John Wesley's Theology Today* (Nashville: Abingdon, 1998) and Steve Harper's *The Way to Heaven: The Gospel According to John Wesley* (Grand Rapids: Zondervan, 2003).

In addition to these general works, there have been many monographs and collections of essays written on specific aspects of Wesley's life and legacy, many of which contain wonderful insights beyond those found in the books listed above, but they are too many to list in this brief conclusion. One recent collection of essays on Wesley's life and ministry that many readers will likely find helpful, however, is the *Cambridge Companion to John Wesley*, edited by Randy L. Maddox and Jason E. Vickers (New York: Cambridge University Press, 2010).

Making It Real

As we have seen, Wesley was an intensely relational and practical theologian. It would have disappointed him greatly to learn that people read his theology and thought about his insights only to put them down in books (or to recite answers about him on a test). Wesley knew that theology was meant to be lived out with God and others in the world. As a "next step," then, after looking at Wesley's life and thought, it is good to think about what kind of difference that life and thought can make to our own lives and thoughts today. Of course, to even begin to apply Wesley's insights would take another whole book. However, even though we do not have the space to draw out all the implications of Wesley's example and insights, we can say something that helps us orient ourselves to that endeavor.

Throughout this presentation of Wesley's life and thought, we have tried to articulate the basic dynamics he responded to and the fundamental intuitions he had that drove those responses. In a sense, these intuitions form the core of Wesley's "theological project." We could try to simply repeat his words and duplicate his methods. However, given how different Wesley's eighteenth-century England was to twenty-first-century England—or America or Africa or Asia—this approach is not likely to produce for us the same results that Wesley had. On the other hand, if we tried to be Wesleyan today by processing his intuitions into our own cultures and asking ourselves what a relational and creational, grace-driven and communal expression of church might look like in our day, we might find some amazing things happening. Our words might not be the same as Wesley's but might still sound very Wesleyan. If our activity were driven by grace-inspired love—wise and intentional love, not merely the "feel good" kind—we would probably find ourselves doing very Wesleyan things. And, perhaps, if we tried to "be church" in a way that accepted people where they were but then pointed toward the amazing expressions of the image of God they were created to be, we may find God responding to our offerings in ways similar to the way God responded to Wesley's. We may not help initiate a revival that significantly shapes our country—that is up to God—but then, we might. Either way, it is hard to imagine that we would regret our faithful efforts to live out the grand vision of the gospel that Wesley has helped us to see.

Notes*

Chapter 1

1. This is when ideas of secular politics began to take hold in English culture, though they had been around for decades before that. For more information, see J. C. D. Clark's *English Society 1660–1832* (Cambridge, UK: Cambridge University Press, 2000).

2. Preface to *Primitive Physick* (Jackson 14:307-18). The full text of the book itself is available online at http://books.google.com/books/about/Primitive_Physick_Or_an_Easy_and_Natural.html?id=fLEUAAAAQAAJ (accessed January 13, 2014).

3. See "An Address to the Clergy," §I.2 (Jackson 10:483).

Chapter 2

1. For more information on Wesley's family background, see Martin Schmidt's very detailed two-volume work, *John Wesley: A Theological Biography*, trans. Norman P. Goldhawk (New York: Abingdon, 1963).

2. *Susanna Wesley: The Complete Writings*, ed. Charles Wallace Jr. (New York: Oxford University Press, 1997).

3. Adam Clarke, *Memoirs of the Wesley Family* (New York: Bangs and Mason, 1824). See also "An Account of the Disturbances in My Father's House," §8 (Jackson 13:504).

4. As we noted in chapter 1, Wesley would later celebrate the Gregorian date of June 28 as his birthday instead of June 17, which was the date that the Julian calendar said it was at the time.

5. Susanna noted in an early letter to her son Samuel that she only allowed herself as much time in recreation as she spent in devotional pursuits (*Susanna Wesley*, 62).

6. *Journal*, August 1, 1742 (19:288), which reflects a letter from Susanna to John dated July 24, 1732 (*Susanna Wesley*, 369).

7. Ibid. (19:287).

8. *Susanna Wesley*, 98.

9. John Hampson, *Memoirs of the Late Rev. John Wesley, A.M.*, vol. 1 (London: James Graham, 1791), 71.

10. *Susanna Wesley*, 235.

11. Ibid., 82-83. The question mark in brackets represents uncertainty about the original handwritten manuscript.

12. *Journal*, May 24, 1738, §2 (18:243).

---

*See pages 10-11 of introduction for specifics concerning note citations.

Chapter 3

1. For a deeper exploration of this time in Wesley's life, see V. H. H. Green, *The Young Mr. Wesley: A Study of John Wesley and Oxford* (London: Edward Arnold Publishers, 1961).

2. Introduction to *The Letters of the Rev. John Wesley* (Telford 1:7).

3. Letter from Susanna, February 23, 1724/5 (25:160).

4. *A Plain Account of Christian Perfection*, §2 (13:136).

5. Ibid., §3 (13:137).

6. Letter to Mary Pendarves, July 19, 1731 (25:293).

7. Letter to Richard Morgan, January 15, 1734 (25:369).

8. *Journal*, September 1, 1778 (23:105).

9. Letter from Susanna, July 12, 1731 (25:291 and *Susanna Wesley*, 145).

Chapter 4

1. The Moravians were a group of German Pietists who traced their spiritual heritage to the pre-Reformation leader Jan Hus (ca. 1369–1415).

2. *Journal*, January 25, 1736 (18:143).

3. *Journal*, March 7, 1736 (18:153).

4. *Journal*, May 5, 1736 (18:157).

5. *Journal*, June 22, 1736 (18:161-62).

6. Diary, August 16, 1736 (18:409).

7. *Journal*, December 2, 1737 (18:195).

8. *Journal*, January 24, 1738 (18:211).

9. *Journal*, February 1, 1738 (18:216). Wesley here is quoting from the official Church of England homilies.

10. *Journal*, May 24, 1738 §14 (18:249-50).

11. Ibid., §16 (18:250).

12. *Journal*, November 12, 1738 (19:21).

13. *The Doctrine of Salvation, Faith, and Good Works* (12:27-43).

14. *Journal*, January 4, 1739 (19:29).

15. *Journal*, March 29, 1739 (19:46).

16. *Journal*, April 2, 1739 (19:46).

Chapter 5

1. Member of the Houses of Shirley and Hastings, *The Life and Times of Selina Countess of Huntingdon*, vol. 1 (London: William Edward Painter, 1839), 34.

2. Spener's book *Pia Desideria* (1675) endorses what he called "colleges of piety," small groups that nurture faith through mutual accountability and support.

3. *The Nature, Design, and General Rules of the United Societies*, §1-2 (9:69). The biblical reference is to 2 Tim. 3:5.

4. Joseph Beaumont Wakeley, *Anecdotes of the Rev. George Whitefield, M.A.* (London: Hodder and Stoughton, 1872), 219-20.

5. *Journal*, September 13, 1739 (19:96).

6. *Journal*, June 11, 1739 (19:67).

7. Letter to "John Smith," March 25, 1747, §13 (26:237).

8. *Journal*, September 3, 1741 (19:211-15).

9. These included *A Dialogue Between a Predestinarian and His Friend*, which Wesley claimed as his own but which seems to rely on *A Dialogue Between a Presbyterian and a Baptist* (1691) by Thomas Grantham.

10. Letters to Westley Hall, August 18, 1743 (26:103) and December 22, 1747 (26:269-73).

11. *Susanna Wesley*, 180.

12. Susanna's death almost certainly happened on July 30, 1742, as recorded in Wesley's *Journal* (19:283) and letters (26:83, 25). However, Susanna's gravestone inexplicably reads July 23, 1742, and so one finds that date referred to often as well.

13. This information comes from Wesley's private journal. His published work never mentions the incident. Most of the relevant journal entries can be found in Richard P. Heitzenrater, *The Elusive Mr. Wesley*, 2nd ed. (Nashville: Abingdon, 2003), 166-76.

14. Ibid., 167.

15. Ibid., 168.

16. Ibid., 174.

17. Letter to Thomas Bigg, October 7, 1749 (26:389).

18. Heitzenrater, *Elusive Mr. Wesley*, 176

19. Letters to John Bennet, October 10, 1749, to January 2, 1750 (26:389-96 passim).

Chapter 6

1. See the journal entries for March 6 and 24 and October 11, 1750 (20:323, 325, 363).

2. Charles Wesley, *The Journal of Charles Wesley*, 2 vols. (Grand Rapids: Baker Books, 1980), 2:62.

3. The two notices of Wesley's marriage, one each in the *Gentleman's Magazine* and the *London Magazine*, give different dates.

4. Letter to Mary Wesley, March 11, 1751 (26:451).

5. Henry Moore, *The Life of the Rev. John Wesley, A.M.*, vol. 2 (New York: Bangs and Emory, 1826), 104.

6. Letter to Mary Wesley, September 5, 1768 (Telford 5:105).

7. Letters to Charles Wesley, January 5, 1763 (Telford 4:200) and July 9, 1766 (Telford 5:21).

8. *Journal*, August 15, 1750 (20:356).

9. "Ought We to Separate from the Church of England?" (9:567-80).

10. *Journal*, May 6, 1755 (21:10).

11. Letter to Samuel Walker, September 3, 1756 (Telford 3:192-96).

12. "An Address to the Clergy" (Jackson 10:480-500).

13. *A Letter to the Right Reverend, the Lord Bishop of Gloucester* (11:465-538).

Chapter 7

1. *Journal*, January 23, 1771 (22:262).

2. Letter to Charles Wesley, August 3, 1771 (Telford 5:270).

3. Letter to Mary Wesley, October 2, 1778 (Telford 6:322).

4. *Journal*, October 11, 1781 (23:225).

5. Alexander Gordon, "Wesley, John," in *Dictionary of National Biography*, ed. Sidney Lee (London: Smith, Elder, and Co., 1899), 9:309.

6. See his letter to Mrs. Charles Wesley, July 25, 1788 (Telford 8:76).

7. Minutes of the 1744 Conference §23 (10:130).

8. Kenneth J. Collins, "Wesley's Life and Ministry," in *The Cambridge Companion to John Wesley*, ed. Randy L. Maddox and Jason E. Vickers (New York: Cambridge University Press, 2010), 55.

9. Minutes of the 1770 Conference (10:392-93).

10. See his *Journal*, November 1, 1773 (22:392) and April 26-27, 1779 (23:128).

11. Letter to Walter Churchey, June 25, 1777 (Telford 6:267).

12. Letter to "Our Brethren in America," September 10, 1784 (Telford 7:237-39).

13. Letter to Mr. ——, October 31, 1789 (Telford 8:183).

14. Letter to Henry Brooke, June 21, 1788 (Telford 8:66).

15. Letter to Thomas Taylor, April 4, 1790 (Telford 8:211).

16. Sermon 50, "The Use of Money" (2:266-80).

17. Letter to Ann Foard, September 29, 1764 (Telford 4:266).

18. Sermon 88, "On Dress" (3:247-61); Sermon 87, "The Danger of Riches" (3:227-46); Sermon 126, "On Worldly Folly" (4:131-38); and Sermon 131, "The Danger of Increasing Riches" (4:177-86).

19. Minutes of the 1790 Conference (10:709n).

20. Letter to John Gardner, December 31, 1785 (Telford 7:308).

21. *Journal*, March 3, 1788 (24:70).

22. Letter to Granville Sharp, October 11, 1787 (Telford 8:16-17).

23. Letter to William Wilberforce, February 24, 1791 (Telford 8:264-65). This appears to be the last letter Wesley sent.

24. Letter to Sarah Crosby, February 14, 1761 (Telford 4:133).

25. Letter to George Robinson, March 25, 1780 (Telford 7:9).

26. Zachariah Taft, *Biographical Sketches of the Lives and Public Ministry of Various Holy Women*, 2 vols. (London: published for the author by Mr. Kershaw, 1825), 1:84.

27. *Journal*, December 15, 1788 (24:116-17).

28. The complete account is given in *The Journal of the Rev. John Wesley, A.M.*, ed. Nehemiah Curnock, 8 vols. (London: Epworth Press, 1938), 8:131-44.

29. Ibid., 8:343.

Chapter 8

1. Preface to *Sermons on Several Occasions*, §3 (1:104).

2. Letter to John Newton, May 14, 1765 (Telford 4:299). See also *A Plain Account of Christian Perfection*, §§2-5 (13:136-38).

3. Preface to *Sermons on Several Occasions*, §5 (1:104-5).

4. So, for example, the United Methodists say that "the Bible is the primary authority for our faith and practice" (http://www.umc.org). The Church of the Nazarene describes the Bible as "inerrantly revealing the will of God concerning us in all things necessary to our salvation" (http://www.nazarene.org).

5. Sermon 117, "On the Discoveries of Faith," §1 (4:29).

6. Sermon 44, "Original Sin," §§II.2-7 (2:176-78).

7. "Wesley's Interview with Bishop Butler" (19:471).

8. Sermon 37, "The Nature of Enthusiasm" (2:44-60).

9. Preface to *Sermons on Several Occasions*, §6 (1:106).

10. *A Plain Account of Christian Perfection*, §19.Q30 (13:178).

Chapter 9

1. Sermon 70, "The Case of Reason Impartially Considered," §II.2 (2:593).
2. Sermon 55, "On the Trinity," §4 (2:377-78).
3. Sermon 120, "The Unity of the Divine Being," §8 (4:63).
4. Sermon 54, "On Eternity," §7 (2:361-62).
5. Sermon 58, "On Predestination," §5 (2:417).
6. Sermon 118, "On the Omnipresence of God" (4:39-47).
7. Sermon 120, "The Unity of the Divine Being," §6 (4:62).
8. Sermon 58, "On Predestination," §15 (2:420).
9. Ibid., §5 (2:417).
10. Sermon 67, "On Divine Providence," §15 (2:540).
11. Ibid. (2:540-41).
12. Sermon 110, "Free Grace," §§23-26 (3:554-56).
13. *Predestination Calmly Considered*, §§47-50 (13:287-89).
14. Sermon 36, "The Law Established through Faith, II" §II.3 (2:39).
15. *Notes on the New Testament* (hereinafter *NNT*), 1 John 4:8. *Explanatory Notes upon the New Testament*, 2 vols. (Kansas City: Beacon Hill Press of Kansas City, 1981).
16. Sermon 67, "On Divine Providence," §8 (2:537).
17. *Notes on the Old Testament*, Genesis 1:31. *Explanatory Notes upon the Old Testament*, 3 vols. (Bristol: William Pine, 1765; repr., Salem, OH: Schmul, 1975).
18. Sermon 36, "The Law Established through Faith, II," §II.3 (2:39).
19. *Doctrine of Original Sin, Part III*, §9.2 (12:342).
20. Sermon 77, "Spiritual Worship," §I.3 (3:91).
21. *Doctrine of Original Sin, Part III*, §7.2 (12:330).
22. *Thoughts upon Necessity*, §§IV.4-5 (13:545-46).
23. *Serious Thoughts Occasioned by the Late Earthquake at Lisbon* (Jackson 11:6-7).
24. Letter to "John Smith," March 22, 1748, §10 (26:290).
25. Sermon 67, "On Divine Providence," §15 (2:541).
26. Ibid.
27. Wesley extracts some of Crane's book *Isagoge ad Dei Providentiam; or, A Prospect of Divine Providence* (1672) for his own *Christian Library*.
28. Sermon 67, "On Divine Providence," §16 (2:542).
29. Sermon 55, "On the Trinity," §2 (2:376).
30. Albert Outler, introductory comment to Sermon 55, "On the Trinity" (2:373).

Chapter 10

1. Sermon 56, "God's Approbation of His Works," §II.2 (2:399).
2. Ibid., §1 (2:387).
3. Ibid., §II.3 (2:399). See also Sermon 61, "The Mystery of Iniquity," §2 (2:452), and Sermon 141, "The Image of God," §I.2 (4:294).
4. Sermon 56, "God's Approbation of His Works," §13 (2:396).
5. *The Doctrine of Original Sin, Part II*, §VI.2 (12:300).
6. Sermon 40, "Christian Perfection," §I.9 (2:104).

7. Sermon 64, "The New Creation," §16 (2:508).

8. Ibid., §18 (2:510).

9. Sermon 69, "The Imperfection of Human Knowledge" (2:567-86), and Sermon 70, "The Case of Reason Impartially Considered" (2:587-600).

10. Sermon 60, "The General Deliverance," §I.1 (2:438-39).

11. *A Survey of the Wisdom of God in Creation: A Compendium of Natural Philosophy*, §II.6.9. http://wesley.nnu.edu/john-wesley/a-compendium-of-natural-philosophy/ (accessed January 31, 2014).

12. Sermon 56, "God's Approbation of His Works," §I.14 (2:397).

13. Sermon 60, "The General Deliverance," §I.5 (2:441).

14. Sermon 116, "What Is Man?" §13 (4:25-26).

15. Sermon 120, "The Unity of the Divine Being," §10 (4:64).

16. Sermon 60, "The General Deliverance," §III.11 (2:449-50).

17. Sermon 120, "The Unity of the Divine Being," §10 (4:64).

18. Isaac Watts, *The Ruin and Recovery of Mankind* (London: Hett and Brackstone, 1740), 5-6.

19. Sermon 60, "The General Deliverance," §I.4 (2:440-41).

20. Sermon 71, "Of Good Angels," §I.1 (3:6), and Sermon 72, "Of Evil Angels," §I.1 (3:17).

21. Sermon 116, "What Is Man?" §5 (4:21).

22. Sermon 78, "Spiritual Idolatry," §§13-14 (3:108-9).

23. Sermon 116, "What Is Man?" §7 (4:22).

24. Sermon 60, "The General Deliverance," §I.1 (2:439).

25. Sermon 116, "What Is Man?" §11 (4:23-24).

26. *Some Observations on Liberty*, §34 (Jackson 11:105).

27. *Thoughts upon Liberty*, §16 (Jackson 11:37-38).

28. Ibid., §22 (Jackson 11:42).

29. See especially the work of Theodore R. Weber, *Politics in the Order of Salvation: Transforming Wesleyan Political Ethics* (Nashville: Kingswood Books, 2001), and Theodore Runyon, *New Creation: John Wesley's Theology Today* (Nashville: Abingdon, 1998).

30. Sermon 45, "The New Birth," §I.1 (2:188).

31. Sermon 60, "The General Deliverance," §I.3 (2:440). The word that Wesley uses in this quote is, indeed, "vicegerent," though it is often misquoted as "viceregent," which means essentially the same thing.

32. *NNT*, Romans 8:19.

33. Sermon 51, "The Good Steward" (2:281-98).

34. Sermon 97, "On Obedience to Pastors" (3:373-83), and Sermon 95, "On the Education of Children" (3:347-60).

35. Sermon 62, "The End of Christ's Coming," §I.7 (2:475).

36. Sermon 45, "The New Birth," §I.1 (2:188). The brackets contain Wesley's footnotes.

37. *NNT*, Luke 15:11-32 [The Parable of the Prodigal Son].

38. Sermon 56, "God's Approbation of His Works," §I.14 (2:397).

39. Sermon 57, "On the Fall of Man," §II.2 (2:405-6).

40. Sermon 116, "What Is Man?" §10 (4:23).

41. Sermon 54, "On Eternity," §7 (2:362).

42. See, for example, Wesley's exuberant description of how the four elements of earth, water, air, and fire work perfectly together in a human body as God made it in Sermon 57, "On the Fall of Man," §II.1 (2:405).

43. Sermon 116, "What Is Man?" §10 (4:23).

44. Sermon 57, "On the Fall of Man," §II.2 (2:405-6).

45. Sermon 101, "The Duty of Constant Communion," §I.3 (3:429). This sermon appears to be heavily adapted from another source, but Wesley completely endorses the ideas it expresses.

46. Preface to *Primitive Physick* (Jackson 14:307-16 passim).

47. Sermon 72, "Of Evil Angels," §II.13 (3:26).

48. *Journal,* May 12, 1759 (21:191).

49. Preface to *Primitive Physick,* §VI.5 (Jackson 14:316).

Chapter 11

1. Sermon 141, "The Image of God," §II.[0] (4:295-96). See also Sermon 45, "The New Birth," §I.2 (2:189).

2. Sermon 57, "On the Fall of Man," §I.1 (2:402-3).

3. Sermon 45, "The New Birth," §I.2 (2:189).

4. Sermon 61, "The Mystery of Iniquity," §2 (2:452).

5. This sermon is a simplification and reworking of some sections from his larger, more sustained defense of the idea of original sin, titled *The Doctrine of Original Sin: According to Scripture, Reason, and Experience.*

6. *NNT,* 1 John 1:8.

7. Sermon 44, "Original Sin," §I.3 (2:175).

8. Ibid., §§III.1-2 (2:182-84).

9. Sermon 9, "The Spirit of Bondage and of Adoption," §§I.1-8 (1:251-55); see also Sermon 10, "The Witness of the Spirit: Discourse One," §II.11 (1:283), and Sermon 3, "Awake, Thou That Sleepest," §I.11 (1:146).

10. Sermon 141, "The Image of God," §II.1 (4:296-98).

11. Sermon 76, "On Perfection," §II.9 (3:79). See also Sermon 96, "On Obedience to Parents," §II.8 (3:372).

12. Letter to Mrs. Bennis, June 16, 1772 (Telford 5:322).

13. Ibid.

14. Sermon 14, "The Repentance of Believers," §II.4 (1:348), and *A Plain Account of Christian Perfection,* §23.Q17 (13:182).

15. Sermon 8, "The First Fruits of the Spirit," §III.4 (1:245); Sermon 9, "The Spirit of Bondage and Adoption," §II.9 (1:258); and Sermon 47, "Heaviness through Manifold Temptations," §III.9 (2:231).

16. Sermon 13, "On Sin in Believers," §§III.1-3 (1:321-22); Sermon 43, "The Scripture Way of Salvation," §I.6 (2:159); and Sermon 44, "Original Sin," §§I.2, II.8 (2:175, 179).

17. Sermon 44, "Original Sin," §II.5 (1:178).

18. Sermon 125, "On a Single Eye," §§III.5-6 (4:128-29), and Sermon 126, "On Worldly Folly" (4:131-38).

19. Sermon 48, "Self Denial," §I.3 (2:242).

20. Sermon 57, "On the Fall of Man," §§II.9-10 (2:411), and Sermon 59, "God's Love to Fallen Man," §3 (2:424).

Chapter 12

1. Preface to *Sermons on Several Occasions*, §5 (1:105).

2. Sermon 61, "The Mystery of Iniquity," §3 (2:452).

3. Sermon 123, "On Knowing Christ after the Flesh" (3:97-106). This perspective also frequently appears in his *NNT*, for example, in his comments on Jesus's full control over his emotions in John 11:33-35.

4. Sermons 21–33, "Upon Our Lord's Sermon on the Mount, I-XIII" (1:466-698).

5. Sermon 20, "The Lord Our Righteousness," §§I.2-4, II.5 (1:452-53, 455).

6. Sermon 4, "Scriptural Christianity," §§IV.1-11 (1:172-80).

7. Sermon 40, "Christian Perfection," §11 (2:110).

8. Sermon 61, "The Mystery of Iniquity," §11 (2:455).

9. *NNT*, preface to Acts. See also Sermon 17, "The Circumcision of the Heart," §II.4 (1:144).

10. Sermons 10–11, "The Witness of the Spirit, I-II" (1:267-98).

11. Sermon 110, "Free Grace," §§2-3 (3:544-45).

12. Ibid., §22 (3:554).

13. Sermon 1, "Salvation by Faith," §I.4 (1:120).

14. Ibid.

15. Sermon 3, "Awake, Thou That Sleepest," §I.11 (1:146), and Sermon 4, "Scriptural Christianity," §I.2 (1:161), among others.

16. Sermon 117, "On the Discoveries of Faith" (4:28-38), and Sermon 119, "Walking by Sight and Walking by Faith" (4:48-59).

17. Sermon 2, "The Almost Christian," §(III).5 (1:139).

18. Ibid., §(III).6 (1:139).

19. Sermon 1, "Salvation by Faith" (1:117-30).

20. Letter to Miss March, May 31, 1771 (Telford 5:255).

21. Letter to Peggy Dale, July 5, 1765 (Telford 4:307).

22. Sermon 85, "On Working Out Our Own Salvation," §II.1 (3:203-4).

23. Sermon 117, "On the Discoveries of Faith," §13 (4:35).

24. Ibid.

Chapter 13

1. Minutes of the 1745 Conference [§35] (10:153). See also his letter to Miss March, April 7, 1763 (Telford 4:208). "Antinomianism" is the belief that the law is rendered completely void by the saving work of Christ, with the result that nothing that we do once we are saved—either for good or for ill—has any effect on our salvation.

2. On the Reformed idea of "common grace," see Louis Berkhof, *Systematic Theology*, 4th ed. (Grand Rapids: Eerdmans, 1979), 434.

3. "Preventing" was Wesley's word, but today that word means "stop," not just "come before," so we use the word "prevenient" to avoid any confusion.

4. Minutes of the 1744 Conference [§22] (10:129).

5. Sermon 3, "Awake, Thou That Sleepest," §§I.3-4 (1:143).

6. Sermon 85, "On Working Out Our Own Salvation," §III.4 (3:207).

7. Sermon 19, "The Great Privilege of Those Who Are Born of God," §III.3 (1:442). Wesley actually creates the word "re-act" in order to convey this idea, since no one before him seems to have used it.

8. *NNT*, Philippians 2:13.

9. Randy Maddox, *Responsible Grace: John Wesley's Practical Theology* (Nashville: Kingswood, 1994).

10. Sermon 117, "On the Discoveries of Faith," §13 (4:35).

11. Sermon 2, "The Almost Christian," §§II.1-5 (1:137-39).

12. Sermon 107, "On God's Vineyard," §I.5 (3:505-6).

13. Sermon 19, "The Great Privilege of Those That Are Born of God,"§2 (1:431-32). See also Sermon 13, "On Sin in Believers," §II.1 (1:319-20), and Sermon 43, "The Scripture Way of Salvation," §I.4 (2:158).

14. Sermon 5, "Justification by Faith," §II.5 (1:189).

15. Ibid., §§IV.4-6 (1:195-96).

16. Letter to Thomas Church, June 17, 1746, §VI.4 (Telford 2:268).

17. Sermon 45, "The New Birth," §II.4 (2:193).

18. Sermon 42, "Satan's Devices," §§13-14 (2:146-47).

19. Sermon 76, "On Perfection," §I.3 (3:73).

20. *Farther Thoughts upon Christian Perfection*, §Q9 (13:98-99). The quote is reproduced verbatim in *A Plain Account of Christian Perfection*, §25.Q9.

21. Letter to Penelope Maitland, May 12, 1763 (Telford 4:213). See also his statement in *A Plain Account of Christian Perfection*, §19.Q6 (13:170).

22. Sermon 40, "Christian Perfection," §I.9 (2:104-5).

23. Sermon 76, "On Perfection," §I.4 (3:74).

24. Sermon 83, "On Patience," §11 (3:176-77).

25. *A Plain Account of Christian Perfection*, §18 (13:167).

26. Ibid., §19.Q21 (13:175).

27. Ibid., §19.Q22 (13:175).

Chapter 14

1. Hymn 136, "Wrestling Jacob," *A Collection of Hymns for the Use of the People Called Methodists* (7:250-52).

2. Sermon 24, "Upon Our Lord's Sermon on the Mount, IV," §I.1 (1:533).

3. Preface to *Hymns and Sacred Poems* (1739), §5 (Jackson 14:321-22).

4. *A Plain Account of the People Called Methodists*, §§7-10 (9:256-58).

5. Sermon 74, "Of the Church," §14 (3:50).

6. Ibid., §16 (3:51).

7. Ibid., §19 (3:52).

8. *A Plain Account of the People Called Methodists*, §I.2 (9:254-55).

9. *A Letter to the Right Reverend, the Lord Bishop of Gloucester*, §I.11 (11:477).

10. Wesley actually credits the devil with perfect orthodoxy, for all the good it does him (Sermon 7, "The Way to the Kingdom," §6 [1:220-21]).

11. Sermon 39, "Catholic Spirit," §4 (2:82).

12. Letter to "a Roman Catholic," July 18, 1749, §16 (Telford 3:12-13).

13. Sermon 24, "Upon Our Lord's Sermon on the Mount, IV," §§III.1-2 (1:541-42).

14. Sermon 92, "On Zeal," §II.5-6 (3:313-14). Wesley borrows this metaphor from a book by James Garden, *Comparative Theology* (1700), but its application here is thoroughly his own.

15. Ibid., §II.11 (3:315).

16. Sermon 104, "On Attending the Church Service" (3:464-75).

17. Sermon 101, "The Duty of Constant Communion" (3:427-39).

18. *NNT*, Matthew 25:40.

19. Ibid.

20. One place in which Wesley gives a clear priority to the household of faith is in the use of money, exhorting his Methodists to loan money to those in the church first (Sermon 23, "Upon Our Lord's Sermon on the Mount, III," §III.12 [1:528]) and to use any surplus they have first to take care of fellow believers (Sermon 50, "The Use of Money," §III.3 [2:277]).

21. Sermon 66, "The Signs of the Times," §II.13 (2:533).

22. Sermon 98, "On Visiting the Sick," §§II.2-4 (3:390-91).

23. Sermon 24, "Upon Our Lord's Sermon on the Mount, IV," §III.7 (1:546).

24. Ibid., §III.8 (1:546).